THOMAS F. COHEN

PLAYING TO THE CAMERA

Musicians and Musical Performance
in Documentary Cinema

WALLFLOWER PRESS
LONDON & NEW YORK

A Wallflower Book
Published by
Columbia University Press
Publishers Since 1893
New York • Chichester, West Sussex
cup.columbia.edu

A complete CIP record is available from the Library of Congress

ISBN 978-1-906660-23-9 (cloth : alk. paper)
ISBN 978-1-906660-22-2 (pbk. : alk. paper)
ISBN 978-0-231-50180-4 (e-book)

Design by Elsa Mathern

Columbia University Press books are printed on permanent
and durable acid-free paper.
This book is printed on paper with recycled content.
Printed in the United States of America

c 10 9 8 7 6 5 4 3 2 1
p 10 9 8 7 6 5 4 3 2 1

Contents

Preface

This book is a study of the ways that cinema represents people who play music. In it, I endeavour to show what moving images can teach us about musical performance as well as what musical performance can teach us about the cinema. Drawing on both media history and philosophy, I hope to make a contribution to film studies and musicology.

Along with scholarly research, my experiences as a musician have proven invaluable in reminding me of why I undertook this project and what were the stakes in finishing it. Like most young males of the post-war generation, I was enthralled by the electric guitar. The sound of that instrument, as I first heard it played by early innovators such as Scotty Moore (with Elvis Presley) and Franny Beecher (with Bill Haley and the Comets), was characterised by a hard attack followed by a quick decay (despite being drenched in reverb and echo). The British Invasion bands of the 1960s continued this approach to the instrument. As that decade progressed, however, a new style of playing emerged that was distinguished by long sustain and a strong, expressive vibrato. Popularised by young rockers such as Jimi Hendrix and Eric Clapton, the technique had actually been pioneered by bluesman B. B. King. In fact, it was by observing King play that I acquired the technique myself. I discovered that imitating the peculiar way the guitarist shook his left hand on the instrument's neck would produce the sonic results I had been seeking. My anecdote is pertinent to the present study because of *how* I acquired this knowledge: I learned the technique by watching King perform on television. After viewing a representation of a musical performance, I gained particular knowledge of how physical movement related to sound.

Our senses provide us with empirical information linking music with the motor activities of human beings. It thus seems curious to me that critics and filmmakers who are seeking a 'musical equivalent' to the moving image should overlook the performer's gestures. Instead, avant-garde animators and classical film theorists have seized on abstract theories that purport to reveal a 'common denominator' – to use Sergei Eisenstein's term – supporting both musical and visual movement.[1] Of course, the Soviet filmmaker fully realised that 'melody moves differently from the movement of a grand piano being shifted by removal men' (1994: 244). That both phenomena can be called kinetic troubled Eisenstein, who, toeing the materialist line, could not allow for motion as distinct from matter. Eisenstein believed he had discovered a basis for synchronicity by reducing sights and sounds to the level of *vibration* as such, i.e. the 'oscillation of particles'. In an essay devoted to expounding his theory of 'Vertical Montage', the director illustrates his ideas by dissecting his collaboration with composer Sergei Prokofiev on *Alexander Nevsky* (1938). After cataloging how he and Prokofiev had explored and seemingly exhausted 'every possible permutation' of combining music and images during the film's production, Eisenstein adds the following anecdote concerning the scoring of a particularly obstinate scene:

> I was totally unable to explain in detail to Sergei Prokofiev exactly what I wanted to 'see' in sound for that scene. Finally, losing my temper, I ordered up a selection of the appropriate property instruments (i.e. soundless ones) and made the actors visually play on them what I wanted; I showed this to Prokofiev and ... almost instantly he produced for me an exact 'musical equivalent' of the visual image of those pipers and drummers which I had shown him. (1994: 371)

From watching the actors' movements, Prokofiev could compose corresponding music that let the director achieve his vision. I want to call attention to the significance of Eisenstein's turning to the gestures of performing music out of frustration and only as a last resort. Was such a connection not obvious?

A similar revelation accounts for the present study, the origins of which can be found in my doctoral dissertation (Cohen 2001). There I attempted to revive a fundamental question that occupied Eisenstein, along with Jean Mitry and others, but today is fairly well forgotten: on what grounds do moving images and music come together?[3] The answer I proposed then pointed to the mechanical movement of the cinematic apparatus: the camera and projector. Once music had to conform to images on screen, time had to be measured very accurately, and the standardisation of film speed at 24 frames per second made for an unforgiving taskmaster. I interpreted the various images of performing automata that appeared on the screen as a sort of return of the repressed; that is, their apparent lack of instrumental (or vocal) facility frustrates the attempt of classical Hollywood cinema to make the spectator forget the mechanical operation of the cinematic apparatus. Analysing these figures entailed shifting my attention from musical composition to musical performance. Finally, my discovery of a considerable scholarly literature devoted to performance *kinematics* gave me the resources to approach the problem from a more *physicalist* perspective. Unfortunately, circumstances allowed me no time to adequately effect this turn towards performance. After graduating, as a professor, I began to overhaul my previous work, pursuing the idea that it is through performance rather than composition that the most intimate relation between musical movement and moving images are manifest.

The result of that extensive revision is this book, whose pages are devoted to palpable encounters between movies and music rather than to the disembodied *music-under* or nondiegetic music heard in most fiction film. Let me explain the difference. In general, music in film functions as a supplement to set the mood or to relay information about a character's emotional or mental state. The source of this 'mood music' rarely appears on screen.[4] In fact, those critics, theorists and movie buffs who employ the term *film music* do not usually refer to onscreen performances but instead to the film's recorded score. Whereas the latter bears the composer's name, in most cases, the musicians who perform that composition remain anonymous. An invisible orchestra transmitting music from some place other than the world the characters inhabit, they are, for all purposes, incorporeal. Should they suddenly materialise in the diegetic world – for instance, as Count Basie and his band do in the barren Wild West setting of *Blazing Saddles* (Mel Brooks, 1974) – their incongruous on-screen presence strikes spectators as bizarre. The present study, addressing a different kind of film music, aims to point out that putting musicians in front of the camera can remind us of the genuine relation between music and the bodies that produce it.

It is perhaps understandable that the practice of scoring 'mood music' might be perceived as simply a matter of finding music that matches the emotional tone of the images and then letting the music play through the scene as desired. This is exactly how Oliver Stone treats Samuel Barber's *Adagio for Strings* in his movie *Platoon* (1986), during the scene in which Sergeant Elias (Willem Dafoe) is killed. As the helicopter rescuing the surviving American soldiers lifts off, the music fades down, with no real consideration for the logic of Barber's music. On the other hand, more rigorous and precise synchronisation practices exist. For example, in what came to be known derogatorily as 'Mickey Mousing', the music's rhythm and melodic contour correspond precisely to the movement of visual events on screen. In Disney's *The Mail Pilot* (1933), for instance, as Mickey's plane leaps over mountains, the series of pitches in the accompanying flute line performs synchronous 'leaps'. Of course, tones do not actually move up or down like airplanes, and the trajectory of melodic 'lines' cannot be plotted along the axes of space and time. For the sake of contrast, consider a segment from Bruno Monsaingeon's documentary on virtuoso pianist Glenn Gould (*Glenn Gould: The Alchemist* (1974)). Here, the camera captures Gould's acrobatics as he struggles to render the extreme dynamics and wide intervals of Webern's *Piano Variations Opus 27*. The film shows visible gestures perfectly matched in time with our aural perceptions.[5] I am suggesting that, in contrast to my examples of non-diegetic mood music and Mickey Mousing, the film of Gould's performance offers a more concrete way to conceive of a relation between moving images and musical movement.

The familiar paradigm for audio-visual music media is the promotional music video on television. My project, however, will not address the music video to any considerable extent because the form generally shows musicians lip-syncing rather than actually playing or singing live. Thus, the genre does not offer much that is relevant to musical performance or documentary cinema. In contrast, the so-called *concert film* pays sustained attention to actual musicians playing music, talking about music, thinking about or listening to music. This degree of attention provided the essential criterion for my judging whether a film and video merited inclusion in the present study. Granted, the amount of time such movies devote to musical performance may vary, yet they share a focus on musicians and on music-making practices. Often, they depict peripheral aspects of musicians' professional lives such as traveling, dressing, posing for photographers, giving interviews, arguing with agents and managers and getting high. Not to be forgotten are less glamorous activities such as unloading and loading the van before and after the show.

Obviously, a purely technical report on the mechanics of playing an instrument would fail to do justice to these complex films. The reader would soon tire of close analyses of hands pounding keyboards and violin bows scraping strings – and I would bristle if confined to such dry subjects. Performing musicians are more than amalgams of disciplined body parts that function as efficient machines. They live their lives off stage as well as on. I have not, however, strained to emphasise their humanity by explaining every gesture by referring to their *interiority*; rather, I have tried, to borrow a phrase from

Nietzsche, 'to stop courageously at the surface, the fold, the skin, to adore appearance, to believe in form, tones, words' (1974: 38). I have attempted to keep the focus on the musician *as performer* as much as possible.

THE AGENDA

I use the introduction that follows to investigate why critics and audiences tend to regard the musical performance film as other than or less than a genuine movie. I link this attitude to a general disdain for performers in Western culture, and I trace this disdain to a persistent dualism that denigrates the body's work and valorises mental and spiritual processes. In contrast, I endorse embodied approaches to music as the result of physical action rather than as abstract forms. Film can reinforce music's appeal to our vision as well as our hearing and remind the spectator of the connection between human gesture and music.

Chapter 1 looks at the prototypical music festival documentary: Bert Stern's *Jazz on a Summer's Day* (1958). Stern had envisioned a film that would transfer jazz from its dark urban setting into the fresh air and bright sunshine of New England. However, despite his intent to counter jazz's association with social deviance, the film fails to banish the racial tensions and stylistic disputes of the post-bebop period.

Chapter 2 focuses on performers Jimi Hendrix and David Byrne to examine representations of virtuosity in the concert film. Racial differences play a part in how these performers' bodily displays signify within the critical discourse. Between *Monterey Pop* (1967) and *Woodstock* (1970), Hendrix had toned down his outlandish showmanship, a transformation owing in part to the black entertainer's bid for recognition as a serious musician. In contrast, Byrne's gestures, which appear alternately convulsive and mechanical but rarely sexually suggestive, enjoyed the status of performance art. Despite these differences, both men led bands that sought to sound funkier and look blacker.

Chapter 3 examines the encounter between direct cinema and popular music in the 1960s. American *cinéma vérité* filmmakers tend to privilege the periods between shows as pregnant with social interaction and personal revelation and devalue performing as mere spectacle. I argue that, on the contrary, rock music performances in films by Albert and David Maysles contributed to the emergence of the figure of the rock star in that decade.

Chapter 4 looks at documentaries that focus on famous violinists to examine how cinema strives to render specific instrumental technique meaningful for a general audience. From a passage in Siegfried Kracauer's *Theory of Film*, I extract two primary strategies for expanding the limited range of framings available to the filmmaker. One is to cutaway to a face in the audience; the other is to employ close-ups of the performer's face. For the filmmaker trying to communicate via gestures meaningful only to a select few, the face promises to speak a language understandable by both musicians and non-musicians alike. Unfortunately, facial expression does not guarantee universal comprehension, and racial and cultural differences remain stubbornly opaque.

Chapter 5 is devoted to a curiously neglected film, Shirley Clarke's *Ornette: Made in America* (1985). Initially begun in order to record the performance of Ornette Coleman's *Skies of America* in the composer's hometown of Fort Worth, Texas, the film gave Clarke the opportunity to realise an aborted project stemming from the late 1960s. Blending concert footage with diverse material gathered over more than a decade, the resulting film renders a dynamic portrait of Ornette's relationship with his son and drummer Denardo and charts Clarke's own growth as an artist.

Chapter 6 focuses on a film of the Sex Pistols' 1978 tour of the US in order to address how a punk rock concert threatened the distinction between rock stars and fans on which the music industry thrives. A populist social movement and a modernist art form, punk issued a radical challenge to musical performance as 'a spectacle in front of silent people' (Attali 1992: 81).

Finally, the book takes a look at the marriage between experimental video art and avant-garde music. A collaboration between composer Pierre Boulez and director Robert Cahen, *Boulez-Rèpons* mixes abstract visual effects with concrete performance footage to achieve a transcendence beyond a single 'real time' mode of performance.

During the time I spent writing this book, music documentaries and concert films continued to proliferate. Moreover, my research unearthed more and more material from the past. I soon realised the impossibility of a comprehensive or exhaustive study. Rejecting the idea of mastering such a large body of work, I elected to approach each chapter by identifying an issue and focusing on one or two films as case studies. I have tried to cover key films and, more importantly, to shine a light on the marginal or forgotten ones. I apologise to those filmmakers whose work I have short changed in the interest of sustaining focus or have overlooked due to my own limitations.

Some of the following chapters address the issue of music and race. Academically, such an approach was at first unfamiliar, yet I realised that writing about American music on film without addressing race was to seek refuge in irresponsible colour blindness. I thus persevered and immersed myself in the critical literature, although in these areas I write as a modest scholar rather than an authority. Still, as a musician, I was aware of the colour line. An aspiring jazz saxophonist and composer in college, and again, a few years later, a member of a white band attempting to break into black radio and dance clubs, I was self-consciously aware of my skin colour. I never felt treated as an interloper, but, then and now, I believe that jazz belongs to African Americans, despite the considerable contributions by whites to the music and the critical literature. I suspect the case with funk, rhythm & blues and soul is more complex still. In any case, the paucity of white artists crossing over to black radio has been exceeded by the extremely selective array of black artists welcomed on album-oriented rock radio.

Having confessed my past as a musician, it remains for me to say a few words concerning the personal stakes in writing this text. In *The Laws*, Plato observes that 'As he grows old, a man becomes apprehensive about singing; it gives him less pleasure, and if it should happen that he cannot avoid it, it causes him an embarrassment which grows with the increasingly sober tastes of his advancing years' (1970: 103). However, the philosopher notes, they may be 'inspired to tell stories in which the same characters appear' (1970: 102). In other words, they turn to words. So have I.

I would like to close this preface with a few words of acknowledgement. I want to thank everyone at Wallflower Press, especially Yoram Allon and Jodie Taylor, for seeing me through the long process of writing this book. Brian Winston's criticism of an early draft prompted me to rethink the manuscript's organisation and improve it immensely. A grant from the Mellon Foundation allowed me to visit the Wisconsin Center for Film and Theater Research and explore the archive of Shirley Clarke's work there. Wendy Clarke and Andrew Gurian graciously answered my queries concerning Clarke's work. The staff at Electronic Arts Intermix assisted with screenings and provided still images of Robert Cahen's videos. Thanks to my mentors Maureen Turim, Robert Ray and Nora Alter for their guidance while I was writing the dissertation that – although changed considerably – provides the foundation for this book. Finally, I want to express my profound gratitude to my wife, Dr. Stephanie Tripp, who read various revisions of this text and lent invaluable critical advice and technical assistance.

NOTES

1 Proponents of so-called 'visual music' often appeal to synaesthesia, a scientifically valid but rare phenomenon. I fail to see how such an anomalous condition can provide the foundation for a broad practice. I prefer to quote Rudolph Arnheim: 'A dark red wine can have the same expression as the dark sound of a violoncello, but no formal connection can be established between the red and sound as purely perceptual phenomena' (1957: 203). I do not mean to imply, however, that experiments in visual music are illegitimate and have no actual foundation aside from pure fancy. A connection between musical parameters and geometric shapes certainly exists. See, on this point, Rolf Inge Godøy (1997), Alexander Truslit (1993) and Neil P. McAngus Todd (1992).

2 The work of Gilles Deleuze is a notable exception. See the chapter 'The Components of the Image' in *Cinema 2: The Time-Image* (1989: 225–61).

3 See Michel Chion (1994) on music coming from jukeboxes, phonographs and so forth.

4 Of course, intervallic distance is relative. We typically imagine two tones C^1 and C^2 as representing the outer bounds of a chromatic scale, with twelve semitones between them, yet we could easily divide an octave into microtones so that a great number of tones would fall between the two extremes. Or, conversely, the octave could be shrunk to a pentatonic scale, leaving only five tones between the two bounds. In terms of physical performance, most adult hands can span a twelve-tone octave but would certainly be unable to cover an octave divided into many microtones – that is, given a standard full-size keyboard. This last point is crucial. Instrument design affects the sense of near and close, high and low. Also, the discourse is cultural and historically determined. In ancient Greece, for instance, pitch was described in terms of sharpness or dullness rather than high or low.

INTRODUCTION:
IN PRAISE OF PERFORMANCE

Don't forget the crablike
hands, slithering
among the keys,
Eyes shut, the downstream
play of sound lifts away from
the present, drifts you
off your feet; too easily let off.
So look;

– Denise Levertov, 'The Hands' (1960: 61)

The poet calls on us to open our eyes in order to experience the *now* in which the music happens, and she insists we acknowledge the presence of the performer, whose hands produce what we hear. If we refuse to appreciate how music addresses our visual sense, we shirk the difficulty – and, I would add, forfeit the reward – of the musical encounter. The media for music reproduction may transform us into listeners who yearn for rapturous release, but the concert film anchors us in the mundane world by placing the performers' bodies before our eyes. Perhaps this insistence on the profane accounts in part for why music critics have continually disparaged the concert film or musical performance documentary.

One important reason that the concert film bores many critics and film-goers is because it does not present a narrative in which changing situations can be traced to characters' motives; moreover, people in these films do not evince a sufficient degree of psychological complexity or emotional depth, at least not while performing on stage. (In subsequent chapters, I show how this results in the privileging of candid scenes shot backstage as especially revelatory of the authentic person.) I link this marginalisation of the concert film with a broader denigration of performers of all sorts in our culture. Considering how we reward top athletes, popular musicians and movie stars with disproportionate amounts of fame and money, I anticipate some skepticism on this point. Nevertheless, the performer's status relates to the devaluing of physical skill in favour of mental work (for example, musical composition), and underlying this hierarchy is a persistent metaphysical dualism.

Despite their popularity with consumers,[1] concert films are typically treated as marginal to cinema proper. It seems as if the more a movie sticks to showing musicians being musicians the less seriously it is treated as a work of cinema. For example, flush with the success of *Hannah Montana: The Movie* (2009), Disney chief Oren Aviv promised that the 3D film featuring the Jonas Brothers would be *more* than a concert film, that it would 'take movie-goers inside the band's creative process' (quoted in Donahue 2008). The term 'creative process' can be read as a euphemism for composing and arranging, considered acts of genuine creation, in contrast with performances, in which well-rehearsed actions are displayed for spectators and listeners. Implicit in Aviv's statement are all the romantic clichés regarding inspiration, genius, originality and so forth. When we examine the rhetorical language demeaning concert films, we typically find declarations that important films take us *beneath* the surface, *behind* the scenes or inside a person's head. We are promised a peek at the operations of the spirit that transcends the mechanics of performing. Consider, for example, *The Genius Within* (Hozer and Raymont, 2009), a recent documentary on pianist Glenn Gould. The film's publicity release promises to shed light on the 'inner life' of the performer and reveal the 'man behind the myth'. Likewise, the DVD packaging of Jim Jarmusch's documentary on Neil Young, *Year of the Horse* (1997), guarantees the purchaser 'the Ultimate Backstage Pass', as if that were the most desirable and advantageous place to experience the essence of the musical event. This discourse is not confined to corporate executives and marketing people but spoken by hands-on practitioners as well. Albert Maysles, for instance, insists that he and his brother David would not have agreed to film the Rolling Stones on tour in 1969 if the imagined result were 'just' a concert film (quoted in Vogels 2005: 74).

MUSICAL PERFORMANCE AND FILM HISTORY

The fact is that film can provide valuable insight into the physical dynamics of musical performance. Take the work of British filmmaker Jayne Parker, especially her collection *Firefox Eins* (2000), which comprises four pieces featuring performances by cellist Anton Lukoszevieze: *Firefox Eins*, *Blues in B Flat*, *Projection 1* and *59½ Seconds*. Parker describes the series as being 'as much about watching music as it is listening to it' (2008). These films represent her own search for what she calls 'a musical equivalent' to the moving image, a phrase that harkens back to Eisenstein's own quest described in the preface.

In a very different context, musician and musicologist Helga Winold has used high-speed film in her studies of cello vibrato. Of course, Winold is not producing entertainment for commercial exhibition but conducting experiments for scientific research. Indeed, it would be utter fancy to propose that, given sufficient exposure, her films would provide pleasure for mass audiences; I contend, however, that this kind of work deserves attention from those involved in the critical study of cinema – scholars, professors and students. Unfortunately, Winold's and Parker's distance from mainstream narrative cinema discourages consideration of their work as 'film' and instead banishes their efforts to the supposedly remote fields of science or fine art. This occurs as a consequence of the prevailing monolithic view of cinema. Our present cultural norm holds that 'genuine' movies must tell stories about characters that exhibit a certain degree of psychological depth. This narrow view tends to reject Parker's work as too arty and Winold's as not arty enough.

Unlike these shorter works, most feature films – musicals aside – assign music less visible roles. Given the demands of psychological realism, even actors portraying dramatic roles seem to lack sufficient *interiority*, and non-diegetic music is often recruited to address that lack. Fred Karlin and Rayburn Wright's well-known manual on film composing, *On the Track*, lists the various roles played by music in the cinema. The first item mentioned: to establish a dramatic point of view; second and third items: to get us inside a character's head or to emphasise an emotion (1990: 48). As the film industry shifted from what Tom Gunning (1990) famously dubbed the 'cinema of attractions' towards the classical style – from spectacle to story – the spectator/listener's focus changed, to use Thomas Doherty's excellent phrase, 'from looking at things move to being moved by things on the screen' (1999: 4). Naturally, directors would exploit music's ability to suggest thoughts and feelings occurring 'inside' characters. A complementary tendency emerged to downplay theatrical modes of representation that draw attention to the performance as performance.

Siegfried Kracauer pronounces categorically that 'music in film must be an accessory to be bearable' (1960: 151). Although he acknowledges many 'successful attempts to integrate musical performances into otherwise realistic contexts', he dismisses outright films that showcase music primarily as 'inconsistent with the medium' (1960: 149; 146). Such hybrids, he insists, do not facilitate the appreciation of either cinema or music. The problem is that the audience, addressed simultaneously as moviegoers and concertgoers, finds its attention split between the moving images and the sounds. Viewing a musical performance on screen, we find ourselves 'exchanging the dimension of outer impressions for that of inner sensations aroused by the inflowing rhythms and sound patterns' (1960: 146). Kracauer thus characterises the musical experience as an inner one at odds with the physical sensations produced by film. He complains, 'We hardly ever listen to musical performance in films … without being challenged to divide our attention between its revelations and the executants – their hands, their faces' (1960: 151). Note that these objections rest on Kracauer's distinction between the 'execution' of music and what he calls 'music proper' (ibid.). In other words, music's 'revelations' must transcend the mutual physical presence and motor activities of performers, which Kracauer treats as obstacles to the appreciation of pure music. Such 'unwarranted preoccupation with the inessential' interferes with 'intense listening' (ibid.). In other words, the sight of the performer's body intrudes on the pure musical experience.

Despite Kracauer's views, the link between musical performance and motion pictures is far from anomalous; on the contrary, it is quite ubiquitous. The cinema's fascination with musical performance is at least as old as the Edison film known as *Dickson Experimental Sound Film* (1894–95). In this modest beginning, we may have difficulty recognising the mature concert film. In a single take lasting twenty seconds, the stationary camera captures Edison's lieutenant W. K. L. Dickson playing his violin into an acoustic horn whilst two Edison employees dance. The film was Dickson's answer to his boss's charge to combine moving pictures with his earlier invention, the phonograph. Edison had revealed his 'favorite scheme' to Dickson as early as 1887 (see Loughney 2001). To those critics who treated the arrival of sound as an apostasy from pure cinematic art, the historical facts offer a rebuttal. As Philip Auslander notes, the invention of the gramophone resulted in 'the replacement of an audio-visual event with a primarily audio one, sound without vision' (1999: 73). Perhaps Edison's quest for moving images was in part driven by the need to rectify the sound/vision schism his earlier invention had brought about. In any case, the so-called 'wizard of Menlo Park' dreamed of presenting lifelike audio-visual images of famous opera stars to those unable to attend the 'live' event (see Altman 2004: 157). Unfortunately, Edison's ambitions remained unrealised during his lifetime. In fact, nearly four decades would pass before the synchronisation of the phonograph and the cinematic apparatus produced a viable sound cinema.

When sound cinema arrived in 1926, the audience at the premiere of Warner's new sound system, the *Vitaphone*, witnessed tenor Giovanni Martinelli singing an aria from *I Pagliacci* and the New York Philharmonic playing the overture from *Tannhäuser*. Historian Edward Kellogg calls this event 'a demonstration of synchronised sound and not of sound motion-picture drama' (1955: 357). True enough, but when *The Jazz Singer* (Alan Crosland, 1927) arrived a year later, it was the apparent spontaneity and unscripted quality of the musical performance segments that struck spectators. This impression was due to the precise audio-visual synchronisation and Al Jolson's casual remarks between songs and not because of the corny dramatic story that surrounded them. It would appear that the immediate demands of performing music occupy the singer too thoroughly to allow him to act (see Nichols 2001 and Chanan 2007). Such an effect, however, raises the question of why one type of performance (musical) should strike us as more genuine than another (dramatic). We shall return to this paradox in a later chapter on direct cinema; for the present, we note that the Vitaphone promised to bring quality musical performances to music lovers living outside metropolitan areas. Still, the Vitaphone shorts were more illustrated records than movies (see Lastra 2000). Their goal was to produce a faithful record of the performance as it would be seen and heard from a seat in the theatre. The sophisticated cinematic techniques of Martin Scorsese's *The Last Waltz* (1978) were still decades away.

BODY, MIND AND SPIRIT IN MUSIC

Musicians lament the trouble musical instruments have in trying to produce meaningful signs and not merely sounds. No one could deny instrumental music's capacity to stir listeners' emotions, but music has great difficulty communicating determinate concepts. The common belief is that music possesses expressive power but lacks a referential function. However, the notion that music refers to nothing other than itself holds true only if we overlook the performer, which is precisely what we have been conditioned to do. In the West, emphasis on music as the organisation of tones in time has obscured its physical kinematic properties (see Shove & Repp 1995). As listeners, we have been trained, when encountering a piece of music, to examine timbre or pitch relations, to imagine pictures of landscapes or seascapes, or to experience refined or intense emotions; rarely, however, are we asked to visualise the movements of the performers. On the contrary, we are often encouraged to close our eyes in order to transcend the profane world of sight and enter the realm of pure sound. For instance, one of philosopher Roger Scruton's chief complaints against rock music concerts is that 'the audience does not listen to the music, but through it, to the performers' (1997: 500). Indeed, rock music concerts in particular insist on rich visual and tactile experiences and promote various kinds of physical contact. For instance, singer Iggy Pop, who has been described as 'intense' and 'dangerous' (Bangs 2003: 206), habitually dives into the audience without concern for his safety.[2] Contrast the porous boundaries between spectator and artist that characterise such events with the formal ceremony of the classical concert as described by Scruton:

> The performers vanish behind their ritual dress, and only the conductor
> – himself in formal costume, and with his back to the audience – retains
> the charisma of his priestly office, while the audience sits motionless and
> expectant, wrapped in an awed silence, and focusing not on the perform-
> ers, but on the music which makes use of them. (1997: 439–40)

I find it hard to believe that anyone would desire a situation in which performers function as mere tools. Scruton prefers a performer who does not detract from our rapt listening by reminding us of the visible, haptic world; he insists that music is an *acousmatic*, or strictly sonic, art (1997: 3).[3] According to this line of thinking, our awareness of the physical efforts involved in playing or singing and, worse still, of the unnecessary movements of the entertainer only serve to vitiate our appreciation of true music.

This ideology is not confined to debates in academia; it persists today in the popular press. Consider, for example, an article by Bernard Holland, music critic for the *New York Times*, who, while admitting that 'some music does bear watching', declares that most of the time 'vision … gets in the way' (2008: 8). Although Holland's annoyance with musical 'thespians' has obviously been brewing for some time, this particular jeremiad has been triggered by a television programme. Holland condemns what he calls these 'melodramas for the eye'. He does not, however, categorically condemn audio-visual media; on the contrary, he even recommends that pianists study films of Arthur Rubenstein performing. Pupils of music, he argues, can benefit by noting and then imitating Rubenstein's upper-body stillness. Holland writes as a proponent of economical and efficient performance, in which a 'minimum of gesture' prevents squandering energy (ibid.).

This efficiency-model of instrumental performance does not cover practices in many non-Western cultures. Musicologist John Baily (1985) explains this phenomenon as an effect of the formidable progress of musical notation in the West, which promotes the notion that the score constitutes the music proper.[4] Certain non-Western cultures, however, do not isolate sonic effects from human motion patterns, some of which may produce no audibly discernible effect yet still qualify as musical. In fact, some African languages do not even employ two distinct words to designate music and dance. For instance, the Igbo term 'egwu' signifies music, dance and drama (see Baily 1985: 239). Philip Bohlman points out that, for many peoples, 'expressive practices do not divide into those that produce music and those that produce something else, say ritual or dance' (quoted in Cross 2003: 107). Likewise, Ian Cross argues that our Western conception of music as organised sound may only represent 'a culturally specific and partial demarcation of the correlates of human musicality' (2003: 108). The work of these scholars suggests that we adopt a more catholic view of the musical event that includes the physical movements of performers and the interactions between those who produce sonic effects on a musical instrument and other participants in such an event.

Unfortunately, a *transcendental* notion of music pervading Western thought and Eurocentric culture has succeeded in lowering performance to the rank of *craft* while elevating composition to the status of *art*.[5] The title of Paul Hindemith's *Craft of Musical Composition* seems to imply otherwise, but the text itself reveals that Hindemith insists that the composer learn his craft merely in order to 'control his hand as to maintain it in unbroken contact with his thought'; the goal is not to develop a virtuoso technique but only to achieve 'such mastery that technique does not intrude itself, and a free path is prepared for thought and feeling' (1968: 12). This process clearly subscribes to a mind/body dualism in which the body is understood as a mere tool of the creative consciousness that inhabits it. Once the composer's mind has trained this unwieldy instrument accurately to transcribe thought into a written score, it remains for the performer to translate that score into music that conforms as closely as possible to the composer's intentions. This widely held, if unexamined, view of composition as a deliberate, conscious activity and performing as a well-honed manual skill proceeds from the division between mental and physical labour typical of modern Western society (see Marx and Engels 1970 65). Those who take an honest look at the creative process might treat composing as a mental skill,[6] but the common view holds that exceptional flashes of inspiration are the cause of genuine works of art. Composers must sully their hands with tonal matter only in order to serve the spirit and the performer's duty is to embody this spirit while corrupting it as little as possible. This attitude can be traced at least as far back as Hegel, who noted with some regret that, of necessity, the composer 'has to give his work over to other hands and throats', that is, to the performer (1975: 936). Hegel insists that the performer 'submit himself entirely to the character of the work and intend to be only an obedient instrument' (1975: 956). Indeed, musical performance as spectacle runs counter to the Hegelian notion that, in art, Spirit strives to transcend its material shell. Musical performance poses a problem for Hegel because, while the tones fade, the performer's body persists before our eyes. Still, Hegel recognises the performer's role in bringing out the work's inner animating Spirit, provided the performer dedicates his skill to modestly serving the composition. On this view, a performer needs to interpret the score no more than a typist needs to understand the words of the text to be transcribed.

However, the performer is not merely a medium through which the composer's ideas are actualised. Performers do much more than simply translate or interpret; they participate in the creation of a musical event. Sometimes they follow a written score; at other times they produce music that arises from a unique situation and defies repetition or inscription. Whereas, before the advent of recording technologies, such improvisations faded into oblivion when the event ended, cinema has provided us with recordings that we can not only hear but also see. This development is cause for concern as well as for celebration: film, a medium of reproduction, destroys that aura of the live performance event as it disseminates the work.[7]

Especially since the Romantic era, we have acquired the habit of investigating how music affects our emotions and thoughts, or, in more spiritual language, how it moves our souls. Thus, the concept of musical movement is analysed primarily through terminology the behaviourists used to call *mentalistic*. Some recent scholars, however, have adopted a more embodied approach to understanding musical movement.[8] Building on the work of John Baily and others, Patrick Shove and Bruno H. Repp seek to draw attention to the role that human motor activity plays in producing sonic events; they assert that footsteps are the 'natural, lawful consequence of the continuous movement of the legs' (1995: 60). In addition, they argue that listeners imagine not only the trajectories of tones rising and falling in metaphorical space but also the concrete movements of the sound's source: 'the listener does not merely hear the sound of a galloping horse or bowing violinist: rather, the listener hears a horse galloping and a violinist bowing' (1995: 59).

PLAYING TO THE CAMERA

Non-conscious motor skills characterise the 'playing' of sports, dramatic roles and music. Although our culture admires physical ability, we still hold reflection and deliberation in especially high esteem – or at least we pay them lip service. The commonplace view holds that composers must cultivate their creative genius, but performers should train to acquire the skill to execute the composer's creations faithfully. As with any skill, the performing musician's knowledge of her instrument must become automatic, for the immediacy of the live concert leaves no time to reflect on which fingering to use to execute a particular passage. Such an extraordinarily trained body can resemble an automaton – a Trilby who requires the genius of a Svengali to elevate technical proficiency to the level of art. The performing musician practices to master the necessary motor movements and then increasingly concentrates on more subtle marks of expression. The jazz saxophonist Charlie Parker said it best: first you learn your instrument, then you learn your music, finally you forget all that and just play. The metaphysical claims of Method acting proponents aside, an actor trains in a similar fashion (and this is especially true of the 'model' actors characteristic of Lev Kuleshov's (1974) and Robert Bresson's (1975) approaches to dramatic performance). To associate the thespian art with non-conscious routine may seem odd, yet the conflict between self-awareness and *photogénie* no doubt strikes us when, posing for the camera, our smile becomes a leer or grimace (see Ramachandran & Blakeslee 1998). Nothing seems more natural than the way our limbs fall in repose, yet actors often do not know what to do with their hands on stage or on camera. The actor – like the athlete and the musician – must train to prevent consciousness from 'kicking in' at the wrong moment.[9]

MUSICIAN OR SOCIAL ACTOR; CONCERT FILM OR ROCKUMENTARY?

We might wonder what interest films that foreground musical performances hold for general cinema spectators who are not dedicated fans of the performers showcased. Many people, for instance, mention the exchange between Bob Dylan and the reporter from *Time* magazine in D. A. Pennebaker's *Dont Look Back* (1967) as an especially compelling moment in the film. Yet no one I have encountered describes the concert footage itself as particularly exciting. In other words, some spectators enjoy the film *in spite of* rather than *because of* the musical performances. It might appear that a musician's value as the subject of documentary depends on whether she is shown primarily playing or talking. Only the latter seems to reveal sufficient interiority, and that attribute is essential for spectators to invest in the person as protagonist of her own story.

Take Bruno Monsaingeon's documentary *Glenn Gould: The Alchemist*. For most of the film, Gould is photographed performing and conversing in a studio with bare white walls and floor, empty except for a grand piano, chairs, and the technical accoutrements of filmmaking. The camera captures Gould oscillating between player and polemicist, but it would seem that only in the latter role does Gould the 'social actor' emerge.[10] We want to know what Gould thinks, and extended scenes comprised of long takes allow Gould considerable verbal expansiveness. But are his words as riveting as the tones he produces on his instrument? Perhaps the former might after all be better expressed through his writings. Certainly, the film's interviews appear far less 'cinematic' than the performances with Gould's display of virtuoso technique accompanied by his animated gestures and odd grimaces. The flamboyant Gould would certainly count among Bernard Holland's despised performing thespians. Ultimately, I believe that much of what might make the average filmgoer dismiss this documentary as other than – or less than – a 'movie' depends on our culture's interests. The film contains no individual protagonist who perseveres, no antagonist who fails.

Musical performance documentaries appear to fall under the rubric of what Albert Maysles has called the 'non-issue film' (quoted in Rippa 2006). While I consider Maysles' disavowal of advocacy somewhat disingenuous, it is true that these films do not, at least overtly, attempt to persuade spectators to take action or convince them of a certain point of view. Still, the much-maligned musical performance film does speak to issues at the heart of documentary, issues concerning intention and the ontological status of the historical referent. Michael Renov identifies the documentary 'truth claim', which says, 'Believe me, I'm of the world', as the 'baseline of persuasion for all nonfiction, from propaganda to rock doc' (1993: 30). Although this statement prompts questions concerning the sort of 'persuasion' the 'rock doc' attempts, the relevant point is that performance on film leaves a record of actual people engaged in the social activity of making music at a particular historical moment. To those critics who require that nonfiction film address social issues directly, this 'baseline' may not suffice for the film to qualify as documentary. For example, Bill Nichols argues that 'documentary flourishes when it gains a voice of its own. Producing accurate documents or visual evidence does not lend it such a voice' (2001: 85). One would have to stretch the concept of persuasion pretty far to cover a film such as *Monterey Pop*.

Clearly, *Monterey Pop* has little in common with 'bona fide' documentaries like Barbara Kopple's *Harlan County U.S.A.* (1976) or *The Murder of Fred Hampton* (Mike Gray and Howard Alk, 1971). Nevertheless, the rock concert film's popularity and relative commercial success make it advantageous to include it under the umbrella of documentary. Brian Winston invokes the 'rock performance documentary' as 'one of the two truly popular documentary forms', citing it as an exception to the dull seriousness of the Griersonian documentary (1995: 255). I might add, however, that rock performance films can be utterly boring for spectators who have no interest in the featured band or in the particular event. This last statement may not hold for the broader category of the 'rock doc' or *rockumentary* in general but for what I am calling the 'concert film' in particular – the film that foregrounds musical performance. My own distaste for Metallica, for example, did not prevent me from enjoying *Metallica: Some Kind of Monster* (Joe Berlinger and Bruce Sinofsky, 2004). However, the film hardly deserves the appellation 'rock performance' since it contains very little 'performance'.

As Carl Plantinga puts it, 'society uses nonfiction film and video for hundreds of purposes; we can no longer think of one as its sole legitimate function' (1997: 29). Plantinga's contribution on documentary to Stephen Prince's history of American cinema in the 1980s begins by bracketing off the concert film along with 'nature … comedy performance, IMAX, instructional, and promotional film' to focus on the 'social documentary' (2000: 370). It is clear, however, that Plantinga considers such a move merely provisional. He expresses this caveat in a footnote, cautioning that the judgements that assign certain movies and not others to the category of social documentaries are often arbitrary. He complains that 'rock documentaries are excluded from serious consideration as social documentaries despite the social importance of their subject matter' (ibid.). I suspect that little of what Plantinga calls 'social importance' is attached to the performance footage itself. On the contrary, it is the off-stage material that appears most revelatory: Dylan bantering with journalists and fans, the interviews with festival attendees in *Woodstock*, the Hell's Angels' violence in *Gimme Shelter* (Maysles Brothers and Charlotte Zwerin, 1970).

Consider, for example, a scene from Monsaingeon's *Art of Violin*, which shows a Vitaphone short from 1926 of Mischa Elman playing Dvorak's 'Humoresque'. (This short film formed part of the programme that accompanied *Don Juan*.) Monsaingeon interviews violinist Hilary Hahn, who makes the following comments on the Elman film:

> If you look at Elman, he's a really, really small guy, with very thick fingers, and he places his fingers in a way that I've never seen other people place their fingers. He has nails on his left hand. It looks like a guitarist's hand, you know. So he sort of grew his nails, I think, to give himself support, so that when he put his fingers down flat ... since his fingers had a lot of meat on them anyway ... he could put them down flat and get a full vibrato swing. And it's really interesting to see that, because he plays with the violin up, his fingers flat, and he's really short, so his arms are very short, so he's playing all the way out here like this [Hahn mimics bowing gesture with extended arms], and he has to lower the scroll just to get into high position.

Over the years that I have struggled to teach students to analyse moving images, I have rarely seen such close attention to detail as Hahn's. Perhaps this level of awareness can occur only when one expert performer observes the work of another. Some might object that this film segment holds only educational value for specialists. Others might dismiss Hahn's comments as merely descriptive, not interpretative – denotation without connotation. I would reply that, before we leap to the meaning *behind* the image, we must look very closely at what appears before our eyes. To a great degree, cinema relays meaning through the behaviour of people on screen. But, if our hurry to discover the *sense* of the image causes us to abandon the referent, Elman's body disappears. Here the social issues begin to emerge, for this erasure is hardly ideologically innocent.

Jacques Attali makes the following cynical pronouncements on music and video:

> Today, the recording of images is intended to be an instrument for the visual stockpiling of concerts and films and as a means of pedagogy, in other words, as a tool of repetition. Soon, however, it may become one of the essential technologies of composition. Television, the prehistory of image recording, did not succeed in giving visual status to music; the body disappeared. (1992: 144)

In what follows, I hope to show how the representation of musicians in documentary film and video brings the body back into the line of sight.

NOTES

1   Although less lucrative and popular than feature films exhibited in the theatrical circuit, the concert film has recently been propping up the flagging home video industry. In 2005, when increasing sales of feature films on DVD stalled, music DVD sales continued to grow, with shipments reaching $561,000,000 that year (see Kipnis 2005: 10). In June 2006 Neil Young's *Heart of Gold* (Jonathan Demme, 2005) placed in the top ten DVD consumer sales, sandwiched between Fox's *Cheaper by the Dozen 2* and Disney's *Dumbo* reissue (*Hollywood Reporter* 2006: 14 XXX bibliog?). In the first few months of 2008, the biggest nonfiction films in the theatrical circuit were *U23D* (Catherine Owens and Mark Pellington) and Martin Scorsese's feature on the Rolling Stones, *Shine a Light*. Box office earnings for both these films look mediocre, however, in contrast to that of *Hannah Montana/Miley Cyrus: Best of Both Worlds* (Bruce Hendricks, 2008), which broke pre-sale ticket records and became the most profitable concert film ever at $65 million (see Donahue 2008). While this news may cause 'serious' music lovers to despair, it points to the genre's undeniable importance as a cultural phenomenon.

2   Those who have not had the opportunity to see Iggy Pop live can see a typical performance in *Iggy Pop Live at the Avenue B* (Serge Bergli, 2005).

3   The term *acousmatic* can be traced to the ancient Greek practice of a teacher lecturing students from behind a curtain, and it has come to refer to hearing a sound without seeing its source.

4   See also Nelson Goodman for whom the score establishes the identity of the piece of music through its various instantiations in performance (1976: 189).

5   See Kant's *Critique of Judgment* (1987). A craft can be taught. Genius cannot.

6   See Margaret A. Boden's comments on Bach in *The Creative Mind* (2003).

7   It serves, in Jacques Attali's words, as 'a tool of repetition'. In *Noise*, Attali traces the historical transformation of music from its function in ritualistic sacrifice through its manifestation in bourgeois political economy as representation, which is characterised by performances of a musical score, to repetition, which offers

consumers an experience that circumvents score and performance (1992: 88).

8 In addition to Cross and Baily, these include Rolf Inge Godøy and Marc Leman, whose recent collection *Musical Gestures: Sound, Movement, and Meaning* investigates music and motion from 'an embodied (rather than a *mentalesque*) engagement with our environment' (2009: 4).

9 A special issue of *Film Quarterly* on screen acting contains an interview with Willem Dafoe. Notice the rhetoric in the following quotation: 'Unlike many American actors trained in the psychological intricacies of "the Method", Dafoe's tasks at the Wooster Group ... required him to be as much of an athlete or clown as a mere interpreter of a playwright's text' (Crowdus & Porton 2006: 40). The representation of the body/mind dichotomy is very complex here. Psychology is linked with 'mere' interpretation, which suggests passivity, whereas the 'biomechanical' acrobatics are lauded as the work of an autonomous agent.

10 In *Representing Reality*, Bill Nichols introduces the term *social actor* as a way 'to stress the degree to which individuals represent themselves to others; this can be construed as a performance'; unlike actors in fiction, such people 'retain the capacity to act within the historical arena in which they perform' (1991: 42). Thus, any absolute distance between a fictional world and the historical world collapses. For Nichols, social actors, like fictional characters, present a degree of psychological complexity, and spectators care about their destinies. In this sense, the musician on stage functions a bit less like a social actor than he or she would off-stage, perhaps because the designated performance space represents a world apart from the historical world. Of course, an enactive theory of performance, which emphasises the dynamic relation between performers and environment, puts into question the impermeability of the 'fourth wall'.

COOL JAZZ, HOT JAZZ AND HARD BOP ON A SUMMER'S DAY

'A jazz band! What could be less filmable?'

– Oswell Blakeston (1928: 39)

Although *Monterey Pop* or perhaps *Woodstock* most readily comes to mind as the archetype for the music festival film, that honour actually belongs to a film from the previous decade: *Jazz on a Summer's Day*, Bert Stern's documentary on the fifth annual Newport Jazz Festival. Although that film was Stern's first (and would be his only) feature-length effort, viewers expecting a neophyte's clumsiness will discover instead remarkable sophistication. Despite the absence of portable sync-sound technology, this earlier film employed technical resources unavailable to either D. A. Pennebaker or Michael Wadleigh.[1] Stern had at his disposal five cameras shooting 35mm colour negative film, resulting in strikingly beautiful pictures and providing excellent coverage of the musical performances. This milestone of the cinema was nevertheless nearly abandoned when Stern, after scouting the location, declared that he had found 'nothing to shoot'. The fact that Stern had yet to observe the musical performances before making and consequently rescinding his decision to abort the project suggests that he attached little value to them. One contemporary review of the film by Alfred Appel Jr praises Stern for 'proving jazz, *per se*, can be cinematically interesting' (1960: 56). However, the photographer's initial reluctance to make the film suggests that Stern himself had to be convinced of the aesthetic value of moving images showing musicians making music.

Aside from his slight experience with moving pictures in the Army Signal Corps, Stern had made his career as a still photographer working in the fashion and advertising industries. Possessing a keen eye for an arresting tableau, he would understandably become captivated by the gorgeous landscape of Newport, Rhode Island. Indeed, the finished film testifies that Stern found the summer's day as compelling as the jazz. Visual distraction was easy to find that weekend. Concurrent with the jazz festival in Newport was the America's Cup Yacht Show, a sailing competition between the United States and England. The film's numerous cutaways to shots of the boating event imply as much concern for yacht racing as for an art form once known as 'race' music. These cutaways evidence a lack of sympathy for the performances that seem to support rather than to challenge Kracauer's objections that films dedicated to concerts are not truly cinematic (1960: 146).

In contrast with Hollywood's treatment of jazz as music-under for scenes involving sex, drugs or crime, Stern offers positive images of music making.[2] Appel praises the refreshing, simple recipe of 'a jazz background accompanying jazz musicians!' (1960: 56). If Appel has correctly identified Stern's 'breakthrough' as the linking of music with the bodies that produce it, cutaways to the yacht race only detract from that achievement. This inference has not escaped Appel, who calls attention to the 'unsuccessful attempts at synchronising jazz improvisation with boat racing'. One of these instances occurs during the segment that features tenor saxophonist Sonny Stitt, whose 'searing, up-tempo solo on "The Blues" [actually titled 'Loose Walk'] is about anything *but* yachting' (1960: 57).[3] I want to ponder this 'anything but' that Stitt's music is supposed to be about. As Ronald Radano (among others) points out, music brings with it an accompanying discursive universe comprised of 'countless other signs and images' (2003: 22). What is the blues about? To answer such a question, we might examine the themes and images expressed verbally through the song lyrics. We find that, in the urban blues, whereas sex comes up often (see, for example, Big Maybelle's 'All Night Long' segment in Stern's film), sailboats come up rarely, if at all.

The point is that, beyond its formal musical properties, the hard bop style Stitt plays calls up a discourse of aggression, toughness and blackness totally at odds with the refined discourse of yacht racing. I want to suggest that we do not need pictures of black urban life actually to appear on screen, for they are already present in the 'anything but yachting' Appel mentions. Of course, the music might spark a great variety of associations.[4] Nevertheless, this broad domain contains a set of gritty images that contrasts with the pretty ones that Stern offers, and Appel hints that the image and sound of a black horn player represents these. Stern claims that he envisioned *Jazz on a Summer's Day* as an alternative to typical cinematic depictions of jazz as 'something downstairs in a dark room'. I maintain, however, that Stern failed to bring jazz out of dingy nightclubs into the brilliant sunlight as he hoped. Those sinister images he attempted to banish continue to haunt this ostensibly upbeat film.

The idyllic setting of this staid New England town seems less suitable for music decidedly urban than for yachting. Scenes of wealthy 'squares' frolicking on the water clash with those of hip landlubbers attending the festival. Who today can fail to notice the exclusive whiteness of the former group in contrast with the racially integrated festival crowd? Oddly, the production notes on the DVD release of *Jazz on a Summer's Day* neglect to mention racial difference, even as they inform us that 'the film offers unusual shots of audience reactions by individuals whose social, economic and age differences over the entire scale from Brooklyn teenager to Newport dowager'. In fairness to Stern, he does point out the controversy that images of blacks and whites casually mingling might cause in 1958, a time that he nevertheless characterises as an 'up' period (see Stern 2000). As a child of the 1950s myself, I recall the decade with fond nostalgia, thanks to an idyllic childhood with a loving family. However, I now understand that the atmosphere of cheerful hope I experienced existed almost exclusively for white males in post-war America.

Racial discord lies just beneath the patina of harmony in *Jazz on a Summer's Day*. Even as it attempts to repress the racial tensions straining jazz at that historical moment in American history it continually calls attention to them. Discord is in fact evident from the opening credit sequence. Following a serene image of moored cabin cruisers, the camera tilts down to focus on abstract images of the boats and the dock reflected in the water. Over these the credit sequence rolls, ending with the word 'Newport' reflected in the waves. This image gives way to a shot of the Jimmy Giuffre Three on stage, revealing the source of the non-diegetic music we have heard playing under the credits. This group consists of valve trombonist Bob Brookmeyer and guitarist Jim Hall along with Giuffre on tenor sax. On screen, black faces are conspicuously missing. What does it mean to begin a documentary on jazz with a performance of three white musicians associated with the 'west coast' cool style? This scene sets the tone for the film as a whole. In fact, *Jazz on a Summer's Day* is marked by a whiteness conspicuous today, after the Civil Rights movement of the 1960s. (Yet how many contemporary spectators would have recognised this?)

For this distortion, neither Stern, musical director George Avakian nor his brother Aram, who edited the film, deserves the entire blame. Like the majority of feature-length movies, the film represents a collaborative effort. Festival founder Elaine Lorillard recruited Stern, who was neither a jazz buff nor a lawyer. He thus relied on Avakian, then at Columbia Records, to determine which performances to capture. Jazz critic Alan Kurtz (2007) claims that Avakian 'literally called the shots' regarding the choice of artists, and Kurtz adds acidly that Stern was 'poorly advised' by Avakian in these matters. Stern does allow for the possibility that 'there was a little influence by who belonged to Columbia' (2000).

Decisions regarding which artists to include required more than musical taste and familiarity with the jazz scene, for Avakian was responsible for clearing the performance rights. Legal complications might explain the film's agenda and answer Appel's query as to why Thelonious Monk is allowed one song and Louis Armstrong four. Of all the musicians represented, it was Armstrong who commanded the largest fee ($25,000). Perhaps the filmmakers attempting to get their money's worth accounts for Armstrong's considerable screen time; however, agreeing to pay such a high fee shows that they placed extraordinary value on this performer. Stern in fact calls Armstrong 'the most important jazz artist there is in history' (2000). Now, although Armstrong's contribution to jazz history is undeniable, by the 1950s, his music was decidedly antiquated, as was his stage act and public facade. The bebop generation had rejected Satchmo's tomish stage antics. As Lorenzo Thomas notes, 'in the bebop era of the 1940s, that old jazzman's grin was not even found on stage' (1995: 260). On stage, young black players such as Miles Davis regarded audiences with a detached, haughty reserve. Neither did the difficult music Miles or Monk play make solicitous gestures toward the audience. (Stern himself admits that he considered Davis's music too 'far-out' for his taste (1999).) 'Hot' was out of style and 'cool' was in fashion, although a cool stage persona did not imply a laid-back musical style. As an attitude, 'cool' provided African Americans with armour against the white world, allowing them to reject the stereotype of the 'Stepin-fechit' Negro hurrying to carry out the master's commands. Unfortunately, as Imamu Amiri Baraka points out, white music critics appropriated the term to represent instead 'a tepid new popular music of the white middle-brow middle class' (1963: 213).

In the 1950s, various 'schools' of jazz were vying to inherit the legacy of bebop, a contest perhaps devised by journalists and critics rather than musicians. The main antagonists fought under the banners of cool jazz or hard bop.[5] The former dates from the Miles Davis/Gil Evans 1949 collaboration *Birth of the Cool*, a project that featured West Coast 'cool' players such as saxophonists Gerry Mulligan and Lee Konitz. Associated with sunny California, cool musicians subscribed to a chamber music aesthetic; their subdued approach was usually described at best as *cerebral* and at worst as bloodless.[6] In contrast, hard bop's strong, aggressive sound was considered appropriately tough for the streets of New York City.[7] Pioneered by Art Blakey's Jazz Messengers and Horace Silver, hard bop bore the influence of gospel, blues and rhythm & blues and anticipated the funk and soul music of the 1960s. Unlike bebop, which had evolved into music to be listened to rather than danced to, it communicated with the urban black working class.

It is tempting to explain the tensions between the cool and hard bop schools as mere stylistic differences, yet an analysis of style should take into account the racially marked bodies of the musicians. The truth is that the critical convention was to divide the camps along colour lines, and musicians as well as critics formulated the difference in racialist terms. Dizzy Gillespie, for example, calls cool jazz 'white people's music' played by musicians who 'never sweated on the stand' (quoted in Meadows 2003: 247). In his book *Hard Bop: Jazz and Black Music 1955–1965*, David H. Rosenthal notes that, despite the participation of black musicians such as Miles Davis, cool jazz was 'overwhelmingly a white phenomenon' (1992: 23). Baraka ridicules the music as primarily 'a kind of white mood music', even as he acknowledges Miles Davis's important contributions to the style (2001: 11).

In the seminal essay 'Jazz and the White Critic', Baraka points out the paradox involving the racial constitution of the music's practitioners versus that of its historians and critics, lamenting that 'most jazz critics have been white Americans, but most important jazz musicians have not been' (1963: 179). Baraka insists on the importance of social context in determining musical expression. The apparent formal differences between cool and hard bop styles actually 'represent not only two very divergent ways of thinking about music, but more importantly two very different ways of viewing the world'; according to Baraka, the 'failure to understand [this divergent worldview] is at the seat of most of the established misconceptions that are daily palmed off as intelligent commentary on jazz or jazz criticism' (1963: 185). Now, although Stern's aesthetic experiment does not pretend to function as social criticism, I consider it a fair question to ask whether *Jazz on a Summer's Day* represents a failure to understand or a refusal to acknowledge the difference Baraka points to.

In a companion piece to 'Jazz and the White Critic' entitled 'Jazz and the White Critic: Thirty Years Later' (2009), Baraka extends the category of critic to include documentary filmmakers. Specifically, the 'brain trust' assembled by Ken Burns for his documentary series on jazz is characterised as 'largely white, mainly unhip' (2009: 151). Unfortunately, complains Baraka, these experts are regarded as 'the paradigm for the intellectual source for any lasting analysis and measure of this music and that is the deepest content of its vulgar chauvinist presumptions' (ibid.). Like Burns, Stern and the Avakian brothers have rendered judgements of inclusion, exclusion and emphasis. Such decisions are not value-free, and these values are represented visibly through the order of performances, the time allowed to various artists and the depictions of the musicians on screen. As Kurtz points out, by relying too heavily on a single expert for musical guidance – George Avakian and Wynton Marsalis respectively – Stern and Burns were bound to commit 'errors of omission' (2010). I think, however, that Kurtz may be wrong to place the burden of blame so thoroughly on Avakian. Various statements by Stern reveal the conservative bent of his musical taste. Moreover, while acknowledging the vital contributions of Aram and George Avakian, whom Stern calls 'a great musical director', Stern takes pains to point out that the Avakian brothers 'did not direct the movie'. According to Stern's testimony, 'all the ideas that make it [the film] what it is are my ideas', and he takes credit for 'decid[ing] what went in and what didn't go in' the movie. In definite terms, Stern insists on claiming *Jazz on a Summer's Day* as his film (2000).

BLACKS, WHITES AND THE BLUES

As the film's opening act, Jimmy Giuffre's quiet, drummer-less trio is the very epitome of cool. In 'The Train and the River', the three musicians improvise subtle contrapuntal lines around the key of D major. Although much of the sonic material comes from the stock repertoire of blues riffs, and despite Jim Hall's bluesy dominant 7th chords and Brookmeyer's gruff, wailing trombone, the composition has a distinct European flavour to it, resembling the experiments of European composers such as Darius Milhaud or Claude Debussy. In fact, Giuffre cites the latter composer's Sonata for Flute, Viola and Harp as his inspiration for forming the trio in the first place. Here the audio-visual medium proves an invaluable aid in revealing the meaning derived from the kinematics

Figure 1 – Sonny Stitt plays the blues

of playing an instrument. For instance, the steep angle of the horn's neck and Giuffre's flattened chin typify the 'legit' *embouchure* of classical woodwind technique. Biting just the tip of the mouthpiece's beak produces the soft, breathy sound called 'subtone', and visually suggests a reserved approach to the instrument. Contrast the segment featuring saxophonist Sonny Stitt that appears a few minutes later. Shown in profile like Giuffre, Stitt virtually swallows the entire beak of the mouthpiece, creating both a loud, aggressive sound and an assertive visual image. Between phrases, Stitt takes huge gasps of air, as if such were needed to support his vigorous and powerful sound. *Jazz on a Summer's Day* invites us to contrast the two musicians, so we should look at the historical context that accompanies the sounds and images.

Giuffre's career began in earnest with his 1947 composition 'Four Brothers', which he wrote for Woody Herman's Second Herd.[8] The original 'brothers' were four white saxophonists: Stan Getz, Zoot Sims, Herbie Steward and Serge Chaloff. The unconventional orchestration of three tenors and one baritone sax ensured that the harmonic voicings would remain close together and tend toward the mellow side.[9] In 1956, Giuffre formed a drummer-less trio with Jim Hall and bassist Ralph Pea, who was later replaced by trombonist Bob Brookmeyer. Soon after the Stern film, Giuffre would start a group with keyboardist Paul Bley and bassist Steve Swallow that played a kind of experimental improvisational music that bore little resemblance to normative notions of jazz. It is impossible not to note that these ensembles were composed of exclusively white members, although this fact in no way proves Giuffre and his cohorts guilty of racism. Over a career lasting half a century, Giuffre acquired a reputation as a 'serene oddity', as Ben Ratliff puts it in the musician's obituary in the *New York Times* (2008). Ratliff's piece indulges in the type of rhetoric characteristic of jazz criticism. For instance, he describes Giuffre's clarinet sound as 'pure but rarely forceful', the kind of qualification one expects to encounter in a piece on a 'cool' musician (to his credit, Ratliff avoids the word 'cerebral'). Yet I would not disagree with Ratliff's assessment. While acknowledging Giuffre's 'European inspiration', he notes correctly that Giuffre's trio could 'convey a sense of rustic, bluesy Americana'. To my ear, 'The Train and the River' sounds at least as bluesy as Stitt's offering, yet, admittedly, it strikes the listener as considerably less forceful.

Sonny Stitt's career does indeed contrast with Giuffre's. Early on, Stitt gained a reputation as yet another Charlie Parker imitator until his switch from alto to tenor saxophone helped him to establish his own voice. Kenny Mathieson places Stitt in the 'tough tenors mould' (2002: 224), i.e. in the company of hard-blowing players such as Gene Ammons, Eddie Harris and the early Wayne Shorter. In the typical hard bop combo, the tenor sax held a place of honour. Mark Anthony Neal identifies 'the heavy-sounding honking tenor saxophone as [hard bop's] centerpiece' (1999: 29), although other instruments, such as the Hammond B3 organ and the electric guitar, played important roles as well. In contrast to the lean, edgy timbre of the alto sax (Charlie Parker's instrument), the larger horn's deeper, fatter tone perfectly suited the hard bop style. The music demanded of players both manual dexterity and lyrical expressivity: rapid eighth-note runs would alternate with inflections borrowed from blues vocalists. The hard bop style combined the complex harmonic variations of bebop solos with the funky repetitions of R&B riffs (and Stitt's performance in the film exemplifies this mix). Baraka writes that 'during the heyday of rhythm & blues, blues-oriented instrumentalists, usually saxophone players, would vie to see who could screech, moan, or shout the loudest and longest on their instruments' (1963: 172). Although hard bop boasted greater harmonic sophistication than rhythm & blues, both styles stayed in touch with the down-home blues tradition.

Jazz on a Summer's Day shows Stitt performing a medium-tempo 12-bar blues ('Loose Walk') in B flat. It is worth noting that this segment featuring

Stitt begins not with an image of the musician, but with a shot of a young, attractive African American woman wearing a sleeveless, blue polka dot dress. The camera tilts up her body, beginning with her white high heels, moving on to her legs, to the tight-fitting dress clinging to her curvaceous body, her bare arms, her ears sporting dangling earrings, her smiling face under a tan hat pulled low. This woman stands among a group of three other African American women. A cut back to Stitt sets up an eyeline match that represents communication between Stitt and the women. They are watching him; he is playing for them. The camera next explores the contours of Stitt's sax in much the same way as it previously explored the woman's body, suggesting an analogy between horn and woman. Stitt wails insistently on a high altissimo note, holding it for a measure, vibrato-less, and then bending the note three times before ending the phrase by jumping to a high staccato B flat. Here, Stern cuts to the woman in the polka dot dress, who appears to jerk forward in time to the rhythmic cries coming from Stitt's horn.

One might argue that these cutaways to the women watching Stitt appeal to jazz's association with the music's origins in brothels and juke joints. The editing calls to mind Norman Mailer's comment of the previous year that jazz is the 'music of orgasm' (1957). It is to such associations that many black musicians such as tenor saxophonist Archie Shepp object. In Frank Cassenti's documentary on Shepp, the musician explains that he prefers the term African American art music rather than 'so-called jazz music' (Frank Cassenti, 1984). In an interview with Fred Jung, Shepp argues that, just as blacks created bebop as 'new music that the white boys couldn't cop', blacks should name their own music.

Following Stitt's tenor solo, guitarist Sal Salvador takes his turn out front. Salvador fares better than Stitt in terms of time devoted to the audio portion of his solo, but his visual presence on screen is continually interrupted by overhead shots of sailboats (which Stern took from a Piper Cub airplane) and close shots of water spray. Separating the segments featuring Giuffre and Stitt is a performance by Thelonious Monk – or at least a snippet of one. Of the approximately three minutes and twenty seconds of 'Blue Monk', the film allows the pianist just over forty seconds of screen time. Shown in a low-angle long shot in profile, Monk is on screen only twice as long as the woman wearing a red sweater whom Stern singles out from the audience – a twenty-second shot that Stern insisted on showing uncut in its entirety against his editor's objections. In contrast to Monk's meagre on-screen appearance, the yacht race claims nearly two minutes of screen time. To add insult to injury,

Stern obscures Monk's solo by overdubbing a radio announcer reporting the current climate conditions for boating. Thus, 'Blue Monk' is reduced to background music for the local weather report. Towards the end of the song, we get a shot of African Americans in the audience: a black man in cap and sunglasses and a black woman in headscarf and sunglasses. A panning shot shows two bespectacled black men with scarves on their heads. We also get a glimpse of Gerry Mulligan, apparently listening intently. We will return to Mulligan, whose appearance upsets the neat racialist categories. The point is that, by disconnecting the music from the images of musicians playing, Stern has turned Monk's and Stitt's blues into 'music under' accompanying white people's amusements. We hope that this is not what Stern envisioned when he declared his intention to transform jazz on film from 'something downstairs in a dark room'.

FROM REVIVALISM TO REVOLUTION

I maintain that the worst offense of *Jazz on a Summer's Day* is not, however, its naive suppression of the racial politics involved in debates over the merits of cool jazz vs. hard bop but, rather, its enthusiastic support for the revivalism of antiquated forms of jazz such as New Orleans and Dixieland. By the late 1950s, 'hot' jazz would be white people's music as much if not more than 'cool' jazz. Baraka dubs it 'a music played by and for the young white middle class' that was seeking to revive 'the still breathing corpse of minstrelsy and blackface' (1963: 203). This nostalgic revivalism is illustrated in the film by the numerous appearances of Eli's Chosen Six, a group of white collegiate-looking young men whom Stern shows playing stale standards such as 'When the Saints Go Marching In' and 'Won't You Come Home Bill Bailey'. One scene shows the group riding around town crammed in an old jalopy, a vehicle that appropriately symbolises their outdated and reactionary musical style. The farcical impression created by segments featuring this group is summed up perfectly by Baraka's disdainful comment about 'young white college students trying to play like ancient coloured men' (ibid.). Today, this group is fairly well forgotten (except for founding member trombonist Roswell Rudd, who does not appear in Stern's film); however, for better or worse, they live on in Stern's film. Eli's Chosen Six provide the lion's share of music during a long narrative interlude (over five and a half minutes) that features scenes of children frolicking in a playground and young men and women drinking beer and dancing on the rooftop of an old house.[10] Intercut with beautifully-shot images of cellist

Nathan Gershman practicing alone in his room, this segment concludes with the group spread out among rocks on the shoreline playing a Dixieland version of 'O Tannenbaum'. Eli's Chosen Six were no doubt 'chosen' for the film by George Avakian – like Rudd, an alumnus of Yale – who was instrumental in having the group record for Columbia Records. Through its association with Yale University, the band became labeled 'college jazz', a moniker that suggests the obvious classist and racialist overtones associated with this revivalist trend.

Sadly, this reactionary stance is also exemplified by the images, sounds and words of Louis Armstrong himself. As mentioned earlier, in the bop and post-bop era, the trumpeter had come to represent the old guard; those jazz traditionalists who rejected the innovations of bebop venerated Armstrong as their hero. In the late 1940s, a war of words broke out between the proponents of bebop and its detractors (the so-called 'moldy figs'), although this conflict owed more to the machinations of the music press than to any actual animosity between the musicians (see Gendron 2002: 150). In any case, Armstrong uttered some derogatory statements about bop, dismissing it as 'weird notes … that don't mean nothing' (quoted in Gendron 2002: 151).

On screen, Satchmo appears bearing his own baggage full of racialist associations, just as Guiffre and Stitt had brought along theirs. As Radano observes, a recording of Louis Armstrong's 'Heebie Jeebies' cannot help but invoke 'the Sambo stereotype, the exotic images – the savage, the ghostly apparition, of Armstrong's early filmic appearances'. In *Jazz on a Summer's Day*, we first see Armstrong from a short distance away, in a shot best described as a *plan Americain*. A tight close-up that shows him flashing the famous broad, toothy smile follows. The first cutaway is to a cute young blonde girl smiling in the arms of her mother. On stage, Armstrong is telling an anecdote concerning his meeting with the Pope. To the question as to whether or not Armstrong and his wife have any children, the trumpeter claims to have answered, 'No, daddy, but we still wailin', to which the Pope supposedly replied that he would pray for the couple. Stern then cuts to two young blonde women in the audience who are laughing at Armstrong's story. These cutaways to the happy faces of white spectators serve to undercut the threat of black sexuality raised by Armstrong's story – as if Stern had inserted them in order to reassure the film's spectators that these white folk were in no way bothered by unwanted imaginings of Armstrong wailin' sexually. Positioned as the penultimate performer in the film, Armstrong thus exorcises any remaining threat of black sexuality evoked by the scene with Stitt and his black female admirers. Such suggestive shots might suit hard bop-pers like Stitt, but 'Pops' must retain his reputation as a kindly and innocent entertainer.

Particularly disturbing is the vocal duet Armstrong shares with Jack Teagarden on 'Rockin' Chair'. A head taller than Armstrong, Teagarden seems to lord it over his rather squat partner. The duet is arranged so that the black man waits until the white man sings his line before offering a response. While it is true that Armstrong is 'signifying' on Teagarden's words, the visual image undermines any subtle points that Armstrong scores at Teagarden's expense. This impression is exacerbated by the camera angle, which renders Teagarden frontally and Armstrong in profile.

Following a solo by drummer Danny Barcelona, the film provides several inserts of young whites in the throes of ecstatic frenzy. One woman in a blue sweater uses both hands to clutch her head, which she is tossing violently from side to side. Another young man in a white polo shirt appears to be in a trance. During the 1920s, when jazz began to influence white youth, prudes feared that the music might inspire wild dancing and immoral behaviour (see, for example, Ogren 1992: 158). By the 1950s, such anxiety had been displaced from jazz onto rhythm & blues and rock & roll. It is curious, then, to see these young people respond in such an uninhibited fashion to old-timey music. The abandon exhibited in these cutaways contrasts to the reserved audience reaction in similar inserts during the Gerry Mulligan and Chico Hamilton performances (see below).

Jazz on a Summer's Day does contain a couple of scenes that illustrate the interracial conversation Radano mentions. The first shows the quartet co-led by Gerry Mulligan and Art Farmer with Dave Bailey on drums and Bill Crow on bass. The second is Chico Hamilton's band rehearsing and per-forming on stage. The single offering from Mulligan and Farmer – 'As Catch Can' – sounds like the very opposite of 'cool'. Far from laid back, it is, on the contrary, an up-tempo scorcher. Following the song's 'head', Farmer takes the first solo. The sparse sound of the piano-less trio allows Mulligan plenty of room to play contrapuntal lines on his baritone beneath Farmer's trumpet. When Mulligan's turn to solo arrives, he attacks the unwieldy baritone sax like a demon. Dressed in a red sports coat, veins bulging from his neck, he rocks back and forth while unleashing an unrelenting stream of eighth notes.

Preceding Armstrong's segment is a performance by the Chico Hamilton/ Eric Dolphy Quintet. Hamilton's band takes the stage in an aura of serious-ness more appropriate to classical music than to jazz. The presence of a cellist in his group might account for this impression. The camera comes in close to capture Hamilton's intense concentration as he executes sixteenth-note rolls on the tom-toms with padded mallets. In one of the DVD's supplemental features (*Short Cuts*), the director explains how he imagined that Hamilton might function in the film 'almost like a leading man'. The comment may sound strange, considering that Armstrong clearly has top billing, but Stern recognised Hamilton's charisma. We hear Stern's commentary on the musician while viewing photographs of Hamilton, shirtless, with a cigarette hanging from his lips. With his handsome face and toned physique, Hamilton indeed looks like a movie star. In the concert film, Hamilton and his fellow musicians are shown wearing matching grey suits, white shirts and dark ties. The look is sophisticated and subdued. At the beginning of 'Blue Sands', the camera pans from Hamilton to Dolphy, who plays flute on this number. During the song, the film cuts to various audience members listening quietly and intently.

Both Mulligan and Hamilton were associated with the West Coast 'school', yet their performances rank as two of the most intense in the movie. In these segments, the stylistic and racial categories truly begin to break down. For example, Farmer, having worked with Horace Silver, could claim legitimate hard-bop credentials. Also, the Mulligan/Farmer band's racially mixed front line works together in a very different way than the Armstrong/Teagarden duet. Farmer and Mulligan appear equal not only as instrumentalists but also as men. In the Hamilton segment, the presence of Eric Dolphy transcends the cool/hard bop dichotomy altogether, for Dolphy represents the film's single nod to the 'new wave' of avant-garde and free jazz then brewing. (Of course, the Miles Davis Quintet with John Coltrane appeared at the festival that year but not in Stern's film.) In the following decade, Dolphy would become famous for his collaboration with John Coltrane (and Charles Mingus), as well as for his own adventurous recordings as leader. Dolphy can be seen on film in Hans Hyklema's documentary *Last Date: Eric Dolphy* (1991).

Stern was perhaps an innocent who was unaware of the feuds between critics and the struggles among musicians for the dwindling jazz audience. *Jazz on a Summer's Day* purports to be a celebration of American music, not African American music. Nevertheless, racial tensions, along with partisan differences over competing musical styles, creep into Stern's film. The untimely cutaways to the America's Cup yacht race, numerous inserts depicting varying behaviours of whites and blacks in relation to particular musicians and, of course, the images of the musicians themselves lend the film an undeniably tendentious editorial perspective.

NOTES

1 Pennebaker had cobbled together six cameras, operated by some impressive cameramen including Richard Leacock and Albert Maysles. Wadleigh began shooting *Woodstock* with 15 cameras, although most of these broke due to the excessive strain on the equipment. Although *Woodstock* was exhibited theatrically as a 70mm film, the original footage was shot in 16mm positive and was consequently blown up to 70mm.

2 Consider, for example, Otto Preminger's *Man with the Golden Arm* (1955). See composer Elmer Bernstein's comments on the score in Berg (1978). As my wife, Stephanie Tripp, pointed out to me, not all jazz films of the 1950s were bleak. *High Society* (Charles Waters, 1956), featuring Bing Crosby, Frank Sinatra and Louis Armstrong, is a comedy in Technicolour and, coincidentally, set in Newport, RI.

3 The song 'Loose Walk' is a rendition of an earlier tune called 'The Blues Walk' by Clifford Brown and Max Roach (see Kurtz 2010).

4 As Eric Porter points out, 'By the late 1940s bebop had come to symbolise, among other things, juvenile delinquency, black militancy, masculine assertion, serious artistic expression, and intellectualism'; nevertheless, Porter claims, 'bebop was never quite able to escape its association with social deviance' (1999: 431).

5 EXXX Meadows cites French critic Andre Hodeir, who maintained that 'Cool was the antithesis of Bebop, a "hot" style that was permeated with energy and polyrhythms' (2003: 244).

6 As Simon Frith points out, 'cerebral' came to be a term of critical abuse and 'energy' a term of praise (1996: 128).

7 'Bebop's vigor seemed to reflect the sociopolitical events and lifestyle of New York City, while Cool reflected the softer, more cerebral side of New York and southern California, where it thrived' (Meadows 2003: 247). Ben Sidran claims that cool was 'played primarily by white Californians', and notes that 'the location may be significant because California is geographically as away from Harlem as one can get within the continental United States' (1971: 123).

8 According to jazz historian Ted Gioia, the Second Herd's 'mixture of modernism and melodicism would come to be known as cool jazz' (1997: 264).

9 The combined tessitura of the baritone and tenor saxophones would give a range from C#2 to F#5. The standard horn section, which includes one or more alto saxophones, adds another major third to the top of the range. This does not appear crucial, but remember that the alto player can perform comfortably notes that might strain the tenor player, because those notes would lie in the very upper register of the larger horn.

10 These last scenes were actually shot in Long Island, New York, after the festival had ended. They were skilfully edited into the film to suggest the festive atmosphere of Newport.

WILD GUITARISTS AND SPASTIC SINGERS: VIRTUOSIC PERFORMERS ON FILM

According to Anya Peterson Royce, Paganini was a mere virtuoso, but Jascha Heifetz was both a virtuoso *and* a great artist. Royce articulates a commonly accepted distinction between technical skill and genius. One of the ways that mere virtuosity differs from genuine artistry, she claims, is that 'the highest level of artistry achieves a transparency in performance such that the audience and piece come together as if the performer were not there' (2004: 24). Despite assertions disparaging the visible in performance, the entertaining effect of virtuosic exhibition depends on the contrast between what we see and what we hear.[1] On one hand, 'legitimate' musical training promotes efficiency and eschews wasted movement. On the other, pyrotechnic displays strive to increase the difficulty of execution without compromising the musical results. Such shenanigans as playing an instrument behind one's back or with one's teeth increase the difficulty of playing and draw attention away from the unseen music toward the palpable physical activity that produces the sound. Such practices run counter to Hegel's insistence that instrumental virtuosity should be 'limited to solving correctly the difficult problems of the composition on its technical side and in that process avoiding any appearance of struggling with a difficulty laboriously overcome' (1975: 957).[2]

In this chapter, I want to examine filmic representations of two spectacularly virtuosic performers: Jimi Hendrix and David Byrne. On one level, this juxtaposition constitutes an exercise in exploiting extreme contrasts. Hendrix was highly regarded for his technical prowess on the guitar but struggled to achieve recognition as a creative artist; Byrne, on the other hand, has no reputation as a guitar hero or as the type of singer to inspire *American Idol* contestants but is praised instead for his talent as a songwriter and conceptual designer. Hendrix paid his dues on the road as sideman for various rhythm & blues acts before finding his own stardom in England. In contrast, Byrne comes from the art school tradition, having attended the Rhode Island School of Design and the Maryland Institute College of Art. His band Talking Heads evolved playing in one local bar in New York City's Bowery.

Beyond these differences, however, both musicians share a history of fronting bands that came to sound progressively funkier and look increasingly blacker. For instance, the Jimi Hendrix Experience began with Hendrix supported by two white sidemen, Noel Redding and Mitch Mitchell; however, by the time of Woodstock, Hendrix's old friend Billy Cox had replaced Redding and only Mitchell remained (having rejoined Hendrix after drummer Buddy Miles had been fired). Talking Heads began as four white musicians but expanded the lineup on the 1980 LP *Remain in Light*. In Jonathan Demme's 1984 concert film *Stop Making Sense*, the Heads' core unit is augmented by five African American singers and instrumentalists. These additions make Talking Heads a band with a majority of black personnel, yet blackness functions as a supplement, in the sense of providing excess and filling a lack. For Talking Heads was a band capable of playing funk yet missing a key ingredient of funk – black musicians.

The public reception of Hendrix and Byrne opens up on a much broader discourse that appeals to the racialist ideologies explored in the previous chapter. It is tempting to treat Byrne as the conceptual mind and Hendrix as the sensual body.[3] I maintain, however, that Byrne exploits his body in performance as much as Hendrix did – albeit in a very different way. Instead of erotic bumps and grinds, Byrne gives us the mechanical gestures of the marionette, the disciplined calisthenics of the military man, and the frenzy of the religious ecstatic. Anno Mungen (2003) interprets Hendrix's performance in *Monterey Pop* as exploring the performer's relation to the instrument. In a similar way, Byrne's performance in *Stop Making Sense* is about the performer's body itself and the relation between its various parts.

I began with Hegel in order to establish the philosophical groundwork to examine the following paradox. Although the audio-visual performance offers a richer experience – at the very least in terms of the sheer quantity of perceptual stimuli – than the audio experience alone, the latter is afforded more aesthetic value. It holds greater 'cultural capital' for elitist audiophiles. Again we encounter a version of the belief that visual images interfere with 'intense listening' of music (Kracauer 1960: 151). The liner notes of the first US Jimi Hendrix album express this attitude quite strongly:

> You hear with new ears, after being Experienced. Those who've only seen him perform only know part of This Experience. They rave about a young man who plays a guitar in more positions than anybody before him. Now, this debut album will put the heads of Hendrix's listeners into some novel positions.

The first sentence describes the transformative potential the music promises listeners (new ears!). In contrast, those who have 'only' seen Hendrix perform retain a superficial impression rooted in the visual spectacle rather than in the music itself. These spectators possess less-perfect knowledge than 'Hendrix listeners', for the show they have seen constitutes merely a 'part' of the total experience. The paragraph implies that the ideal way to appreciate Hendrix's music is without the performer's distracting activities. The purified listening experience has the capability not only to affect ears but to influence 'heads', i.e. to affect minds.

Of course, the liner notes exist to promote the LP – to extol the wonders of modern recording technology – and not to alert the consumer that it is perhaps the audio recording rather than the audio-visual performance that renders only a piece of a richer totality. Despite some notable exceptions, the rock music industry became enormously successful by selling vinyl through radio play; consequently, rock is primarily an audio phenomenon.[4] However, I want to draw attention to a couple of instances that belie this claim: the Jimi Hendrix Experience's performance of 'Wild Thing' in D. A. Pennebaker's *Monterey Pop* and Hendrix's version of 'The Star-Spangled Banner' in Michael Wadleigh's *Woodstock*.

Despite their weighty status in the guitarist's corpus, neither song appears on Hendrix's studio LPs; rather, they exist for all purposes on screen. Clearly, film has played a significant role in constructing the public image of such a visually compelling performer as Hendrix. These two films represent two poles in the musician's changing approach to performance over the course of two years. At Monterey, Hendrix appears as a magician, an acrobat, who dazzles the audience by playing his instrument behind his back, with his teeth, with one hand, and who concludes the set by burning his guitar. In contrast, at

Woodstock, Hendrix offers up a relatively sedate performance. We detect an important transformation: the outrageous showman has changed into a serious musician. I want to suggest that the two films indicate – they do not exactly prove, I admit – that such a transformation had indeed occurred or had begun to occur. Whereas the 'Wild Thing' performance is trivial, entertaining and – to use a clichéd term that nonetheless suits my purposes – *carnivalesque*, 'The 'Star-Spangled Banner' is the work of an earnest social critic.[5]

The audio commentary by Charles Shaar Murray on the DVD *Jimi Plays Monterey* invokes this transformation:

> There are very few of Hendrix's major film performances in the later stages of his career where he really bothers to do that stuff anymore because what he figured was that once he had the audience's attention he could concentrate on what he really wanted him to do which was play music. But, unfortunately, a lot of his audiences were stuck at that stage.

According to Murray, Hendrix wanted to abandon the attention-getting gestures once they had served their purpose. That they persisted is the result of the philistine audience's refusal to allow the artist to grow. Similar to Murray, Eric Clapton claims that such moves were Hendrix's way of 'testing' the audience. 'If they're digging it', Clapton claims, 'he won't like the audience' (quoted in Waksman 2001: 197). Rather than a reliable account of actual circumstances, that last statement more likely reflects Clapton's wish to present Hendrix as a musician's musician. It also resembles Murray's attempt to link the images on screen to the musician's mental state.

Hendrix's subdued attitude onstage at Woodstock very likely proceeded from his dismay at having to perform at eight o'clock in the morning the day after the festival had officially ended. James Parker (2009) has pointed to a combination of various drugs as contributing to the relatively laid-back performance. Whatever cause the biographical facts may imply, another possibility leaps out from the critical discourse on Hendrix's career. For this pop star, critical acclaim required a transformation from sensational freak to dignified musician: Hendrix would have to suppress or even abandon his stage antics. The public reception of black performers can account to a significant degree for the difference between Hendrix's two performances in these films.

A reading of the critical discourse offers the opportunity to show how the invisible spirit is valued at the expense of the phenomenal physical being (that is, the being as it appears either as an immediate presence or as a likeness in media). Hendrix's outrageous moves rankled people who objected not only to the sight of the performer but also to the supposedly superfluous gestures that signify mere showmanship. It seems that, as Hendrix biographer David Henderson reports, 'everyone ... hated [the flamboyant stage movement], except the fans' (2008: 339), who, we have seen, are often reviled as failing to understand the artist's need to evolve. In Hendrix's case, these fans were mostly young white hippies. I want to point out, however, that not all of the latter appreciated Hendrix's theatrics. As Philip Auslander (2006) observes, the 1960s counterculture harboured a suspicion toward theatricality as patently inauthentic. For instance, the choreographed dance moves and extravagant costumes of many soul groups seemed too close to the old show-biz entertainment of their parent's generation. In contrast, concerts by psychedelic groups were characterised by a 'typically low-key performance style' (Auslander 2006: 18). In the counterculture's emphasis on concentrated, meditative listening, Auslander detects a definite 'antiocular bias' (2006: 19).

Much of the critical animosity directed at Hendrix can be traced to racial issues. However, the tension is neither strictly nor primarily interracial, because Hendrix angered and alienated not only whites but African Americans as well. Not anomalous in this regard, Hendrix was one of many black musicians who, in order to gain middle-class recognition as artists, needed to 'alter their public image as *performers*' (Baraka 1963: 173; emphasis in original). To undo the stigma of minstrelsy, they needed to wipe away any traces of blackface make-up. Unfortunately, many perceived Hendrix as pandering to white notions of black entertainers (see Saunders 2007). For instance, after witnessing Hendrix at Monterey, music critic Robert Christgau (1969) labeled him 'a psychedelic Uncle Tom' and rendered a negative judgment of the performance as a whole. The sexually suggestive sexual acrobatics of the show clearly troubled Christgau, who complains that Hendrix 'was loud with his teeth and behind his back and between his legs'. The article's tone and vocabulary reveal a strident anxiety apparently caused by public shows of black masculinity and boasts of sexual prowess. Christgau can only grudgingly allow that the guitarist's performance might be redeemed as a 'vulgar parody of rock theatrics'. Yet he praises The Who for their theatrics, which he legitimises as authentically derived from their 'lower-class stance', a social position radically non-bourgeois but still comfortably white.

The British, according to Christgau, have a mania for the 'Real Thing', by which he means genuine *black* rhythm & blues. Hendrix, however, he accuses of somehow faking it – of not being sincere. Similar suspicions of insincerity plagued modern blues players like Buddy Guy, an extrovert performer who influenced Hendrix.[6] As Baraka points out, the black middle class regarded rhythm & blues as an embarrassment, in part because R&B could be 'more easily *faked*'. 'One gets the idea that a man who falls down on his back screaming is doing so, even though he might be genuinely moved to do so, more from a sense of performance than from any unalterable emotional requirement' (1963: 173).[7]

David Henderson relates a story about the New Years Eve show at the Fillmore East that produced the tracks that would become the 'Band of Gypsys' album. Bill Graham relates how he told Hendrix that his acrobatics 'slowed and stumbled the music' even if they wowed the crowd, which actually failed to appreciate the music for itself. Unlike the undiscriminating audience, Gra-ham's location 'behind the stage only hearing the concert' produced a very different, dissatisfying, experience (2008: 338). His supposedly keener awareness and superior musical taste left him wanting more. The promoter then indulged in a bit of plain talking that angered the guitarist yet prompted him to play the second set of that night's show standing 'rock still' (2008: 339). This change resulted in musical precision that rendered the tracks used for the record. Certainly, increased attention paid to the mechanics of producing the sound will yield a superior recording. Yet the rhetoric reveals a paradox that, in the second set, Hendrix gives Graham – and presumably the audience – 'more' by giving them less. That is, more music, but less entertainment. According to this logic, spectacle and music form part of a zero sum game in which gains of the former imply loss for the latter.

A quick glance at the chronology of events, however, reveals that Graham's heart-to-heart with Hendrix could not be the catalyst for change in the latter's performance style. The Fillmore East performance of 'Band of Gypsys' occurred on New Years Eve 1969, whereas the Woodstock festival took place in August 1969. Of course, not just any year bridged 1967 and 1969. The murders of Bobby Kennedy and Martin Luther King Jr, Richard Nixon's election as president of the US, the police riot during the Democratic National Convention in Chicago, and increasing police harassment of the Black Panther Party are just a few of the events that mark 1968 as extraordinary. Such social turmoil was bound to affect Hendrix's approach to his music, prompting an increased seriousness of purpose.

FROM MONTEREY TO WOODSTOCK

The audio-visual evidence in the films allows us to see and hear what the historical documents and anecdotes report. Recall that Murray claims to detect a trend towards increasingly staid performances in the films. I believe he is correct despite the fact that the late performances on film do not present a consistent portrait of Hendrix as a performer. To my mind, the hyperactive performances in Peter Pilafian's *Jimi Plays Berkeley* (1971), culled from a pair of shows in May 1970,[8] simply show an exhausted Hendrix desperately trying to overcome his lack of enthusiasm for the power trio format and his disdain for an undiscriminating audience. Then again Murray Lerner's film *Jimi Hendrix at the Isle of Wight* (1991) presents a considerably less energetic performer. I think that by citing the 'major' films, Murray is referring to *Monterey Pop* and *Woodstock*. In any case, the work of Pennebaker and Wadleigh will remain important not just to Jimi Hendrix fans but to people interested in the history of cinema. As canonical films, these works will provide our focus here.

Pennebaker regarded *Monterey Pop* (and not his film of Bob Dylan's 1965 English tour, *Dont Look Back*) as his first concert film. The filmmaker avers that, when he shot Monterey, he had never seen a concert film. He thus saw himself as pioneering a new genre of documentary. Wadleigh, on the other hand, did not set out to make a concert film since the Woodstock event was intended as something other than a concert – An Aquarian Exposition: Three Days of Peace and Music. Much of the style of *Woodstock* proceeds from Wadleigh's predilection for social and political issues; he describes himself back then as a *verité*-style filmmaker immersed in social issues,[9] who was hoping 'to do a *magnum opus* on blacks in America' (NHPR interview 2004). To apply for the job, he showed his film of Aretha Franklin, which used multiple cameras for split-screen effects. The festival's organisers were impressed by Wadleigh's politically engaged and formally innovative work.

Despite the split-screen effects employed throughout the *Woodstock* film, however, 'The Star-Spangled Banner' is rendered in one 3'45" shot taken by Wadleigh himself. Although Pennebaker boasts about how he resisted interrupting the footage captured by cameraman Jim Desmond with cutaways, 'Wild Thing' actually contains quite a few cuts, especially in contrast to the truly extraordinary long take of Hendrix in *Woodstock*. A lack of B-roll footage may be responsible for this single-shot approach of the latter film: by the time Hendrix took the stage, only two cameras (out of fifteen) remained in working order.

The sequence begins with a wide shot of the performers from the rear of the stage. This image is gradually replaced by a superimposed shot of Hendrix in medium close-up. The camera zooms in to capture Hendrix's face in tight close-up, revealing the expressive grimaces during the scene when the guitarist creates sonic effects that mimic 'bombs bursting'. For the remainder of the song, the camera either focuses closely on Hendrix's hands on the whammy bar and the guitar neck or zooms out slightly to catch his facial expression. All of this is rendered in a single take: there are no cuts.

Although he adored Hendrix's rendition of 'The Star-Spangled Banner', in Wadleigh's estimation, the remainder of the set 'sucked' because, he recalls, 'it was jazz' and not 'kick-ass rock & roll' (quoted in Roby 2002: 244). Wadleigh's opinion makes a valid point about the kind of musical snobbery that privileges jazz as more complex and sophisticated than simplistic rock. Musicians can internalise this middlebrow elitism, and many players have spoiled a straightforward and clean style by introducing pretentiously baroque elements. However, reactions superficially similar to Wadleigh's might be traced to a more sinister, racist ideology. White audiences expected Hendrix, as a black performer, to embody the physical and sensual, and some spectators would find a more sober performance disappointing (see Frith 1996).

A similar charge had been leveled at bebop musicians: they had lost touch with the taste of the masses. The flip side of the bourgeois yearning for sophistication and legitimacy is what Ted Gioia calls the primitivist myth of black music. This myth regards formal training and technical proficiency as obstacles to natural vitality and enthusiasm. Gioia complains that these romanticise the dangerous elements of jazz legend:

> That the various well-publicised excesses of the jazz musician's personal life are not problems to be avoided but signs that the musician has achieved a special intensity of existence that sets him apart from his peers. ... Restraint, discipline, reflection, self-criticism are for artists in the decadent Western tradition, and have little to do with primitive art and, by implication, with jazz. (1998: 143)

In 1928, Oswell Blakeston, the editor of the film journal *Close Up*, complained of 'the ridiculous positions in which ... actresses hold the violin ... or the amazing way in which hands thump piano keys in close-ups' (1928: 41). Even then, spectators expected representational fidelity. Of course, some performances are supposed be 'amazing' and occasionally, ridiculous as well.

Blakeston objects to the practice of putting a jazz band on screen because, he argues, such efforts invariably fail to capture 'the dynamic force of negro vitality' (1928: 39).

OSTENTATION VIRTUOSITY

In his article on the politics of bebop, Eric Lott calls virtuosity the young black jazz musician's 'best weapon' in the struggle of mind against circumstance (1995: 243). Some of those circumstances were broadly social and others narrowly musical. The younger players itched to break free from the constraints imposed by the arrangers' charts that lay open on their music stands. In after-hours jam sessions and cutting contests, musicians were allowed to – or, more accurately, compelled to – flaunt that technical proficiency they were obliged to repress in their regular band jobs.

Clint Eastwood's biopic on Charlie Parker, *Bird* (1988), not only celebrates Parker's extraordinary talent but also revels in telling the sordid tale of his dissipation. Following the credits, we get a backstage view of Parker (Forest Whittaker) on the bandstand playing a blistering rendition of 'Lester Leaps In', an up-tempo number that introduces the spectator to Parker's virtuosity. The setting depicts the atmosphere of a nightclub in New York City of the 1940s. Shots of the band are interspersed with those of an appreciative audience of rowdy sailors and fashionably dressed women. The camera travels slowly around to position itself directly in front of the saxophonist. Our first glimpse of the adult Parker reveals a man possessed. Dressed in a suit and tie, he has a stocky build and a coffee complexion, his face slick with sweat. A close-up of Parker's left hand shows his fingers virtually flying across the keys of his instrument. In fact, his entire upper body is in frenetic motion – his shoulders moving, his left elbow jutting out spastically. While such a kinetic portrait may provide a compelling scene for a Hollywood biopic, the fact is that, as Scott DeVeaux reports, Parker 'stood unnervingly still while he played' (1997: 173; see also Gabbard 1996: 87–9). Indeed, the few feet of extant documentary footage of Parker performing confirms his serene attitude on stage. We wonder to what extent racial stereotyping accounts for this uncharacteristically animated portrayal of Parker. Stanley Crouch, who objects that Forest Whitaker 'has been instructed to jump and jerk and thrust his horn outward, exactly as Parker did not' (1998: 253), detects a pervasive negative racial stereotyping throughout Eastwood's movie. Crouch complains that Eastwood 'reduces the complexities of the Afro-American world to a dark, rainy pit in which negroes sweat, suffer, dance a little, mock each other, make music, and drop dead, releasing at last a burden of torment held at bay only by drugs' (1998: 252).

Although moving-image footage of Parker is rare, his occasional band mate Dizzy Gillespie has been the subject of several documentaries, including the debut film from documentarian Les Blank. Blank shows us Gillespie the entertainer, the man known for his on-stage antics – for instance, introducing the band to one another instead of to the audience – as well as for his virtuosic trumpet playing. On stage John Birks Gillespie would transform himself into Dizzy, a stage persona largely responsible for the iconography of the hipster: glasses, goatee, beret, smart clothes.[10] Add to this Gillespie's unorthodox technique – he puffed his cheeks out when he played – and his bent horn, and he cut quite a figure in person and in pictures. Eric Porter claims that, for Gillespie, 'bebop meant artistic seriousness, but it also meant playing the role of the entertainer' (1999: 442).

Unlike Parker, composer and pianist Thelonious Monk managed to avoid hard drugs; unfortunately, he lacked Gillespie's ability to negotiate the 'square' world. Monk suffered bouts of bizarre behaviour that bordered on dementia and sometimes required his hospitalisation. His eccentricities are apparent in Charlotte Zwerin's *Straight, No Chaser* (1988), which begins with Monk twirling around onstage. 'Unconventional' would be the polite word to describe Monk's piano technique. Fingers splayed flat, he attacks the instrument; suddenly, his fingers leap off the keys. In solo pieces, his left hand might break into a slow but steady stride that betrays his familiarity with a range of jazz styles. Occasionally, he hesitates, hands poised above the keys, as if he were unsure of what chord to play next. Watching Monk play produces anxiety for spectators, who remain unsure of which chord will come next or whether the performer might become vociferously rude or stubbornly mute.

HOW DO I WORK THIS?

Whereas Thelonious Monk's weird behaviour on stage earned him a reputation as brilliant but *damaged*, David Byrne's bizarre spasms have been easily subsumed within the tradition of performance art. Talking Heads also escaped the stigma attached to the 'punk rock' label. Indeed, in contrast to other bands that emerged from New York City's punk scene at CBGB's – the Ramones, Television, Dead Boys and Blondie – Talking Heads appeared more artsy than gritty, more brainy than sexy. Byrne avoided the rock 'n' roll attitude and stoned look of Stiv Bators or Johnny Thunders, adopting instead the public persona of a shy, nervous college boy reluctantly performing his songs at a frat party. Demme remembers an early performance in which the band played through its set mechanically, 'like robots'. Early footage of Talking Heads performing at CBGB's in Amos Poe and Ivan Kral's *Blank Generation* (1976) confirms Demme's observation. Here, the performers appear downright uncomfortable on stage. Byrne's eyes remain riveted on his guitar's fretboard as he sings, and bassist Tina Weymouth, equally absorbed in playing her instrument, hardly moves.

In the 1980s, however, Talking Heads would develop into one of the most visually compelling bands on early MTV. (What could be more suitable for television than talking heads?) Talking Heads' unique music videos contributed greatly to their success and helped to distinguish them from the plethora of 'new wave' bands emerging in the late 1970s and early 1980s. Unlike, say, the B-52s, Talking Heads could be taken seriously as 'art' and not dismissed as kitsch. Byrne's quirky persona worked well on the small screen. In 'Burnin' Down the House', his ghostly face gazes blankly out of the screen. In many scenes, he leads the band in upper-body bends and shoulder shrugs atop stiff legs. In the video for 'Once in a Lifetime' (choreographed by Toni Basil), Byrne appears lost in a trance or suffering from a seizure, his body occasionally buffeted by invisible forces.

The style of the music videos influenced the stage show as it appears in Demme's film of the Talking Heads concert tour 'Stop Making Sense'. Truly deserving the designation 'concert film', *Stop Making Sense* contains no interviews, no backstage revelations and practically no cutaways to audience reactions. Demme used eight cameras to film the show. The wide-angle distant shots work well to capture the high-energy synchronised calisthenics that reach their climax with the entire band jogging in place in 'Life During Wartime'. (As Byrne says, *Stop Making Sense* could function as an aerobics video if the viewer followed his moves.) The band offers an undeniably energetic performance, which is, at the same time, oddly lacking in sensuality. Consider, for example, the most recognisable icon of the show: Byrne's oversized suit. In the self-interview featured on the DVD, the singer explains that the big suit was intended to make the head smaller. Such a change of proportion could be interpreted as symbolising a shift from mind to muscle. However, the shrinking of the head does not simultaneously emphasise the torso and limbs. The oversized suit hides the singer's body even as it enlarges Byrne's presence on stage. His movements no longer appear athletic but, rather, mechanical – the dance of a marionette.

In 'Once in a Lifetime', Byrne performs untrammeled by the guitar, freeing him from worries over how his spastic bodily gestures might affect the sound. With outstretched arms he 'blesses' the audience during the song's choruses and shakes his entire body during an instrumental break. None of these gestures come across as erotic, unlike Hendrix's simulated intercourse with his guitar. Byrne often resembles an epileptic having a seizure or a mystic in a trance. Whereas Hendrix treats his guitar as a sexual member, Byrne appears ill at ease even with his body's flesh-and-blood appendages. In the second verse of the song, for example, the singer asks 'how do I work this?', clenching and unclenching his fist while alternately extending and contracting his arm. His limbs resist obeying the commands of his mind.

'Once in a Lifetime' does not employ the structure of a conventional pop song in which a melody is sung over chord changes. Instead, like most of the other pieces on the 'Remain in Light' LP, the song was composed by layering vocals, guitars, keyboards and percussion over a looped rhythm track. Consequently, verse, chorus and bridge occur as minimal variations on top of a monotonous (but effectively funky) sparse bass line and no-frills drumbeat. On this foundation, Byrne preaches to his 'congregation' and leads them in sing-along choruses. This structure provides an opportunity for the filmmaker to cut between performers as they enter and exit, but, for the most part, Demme rejects this option to focus on Byrne alone. After all, this is Byrne's *tour de force* performance, which the popular music video has made famous. The segment begins with a shot of Bernie Worrell, dressed in a sleeveless white t-shirt, glowing in the beam of a white spotlight, triggering the song's signature synthesizer arpeggio on his Prophet V. The camera then pans over to Byrne, dressed in a baggy suit and wearing glasses, an outfit that recalls his garb in the 'Once in a Lifetime' music video. For most of the song, the camera will maintain this frontal shot of Byrne, with drummer Chris Frantz barely visible over the singer's left shoulder. At about four minutes into the song, however, when the vocalist pauses and the band begins the three-chord vamp that signals the song's finale, the camera tilts down slightly to isolate Byrne, who bends his upper torso slowly backwards and holds that position. A shot of the phallic microphone stand seemingly protruding from his crotch provides the song's lone sexually-charged image. After eight bars of the instrumental groove, the singer bolts upright. The film then cuts to what is perhaps its most powerful tableau – its effect owing in part to the relief it provides from the focus on Byrne. The camera angle shifts from its frontal

Figure 2 – David Byrne as evangelist

position to an approximately 45-degree angle, revealing four other musicians on stage with Byrne. The stage design has divided the frame horizontally into two levels. Atop the keyboard riser, Jerry Harrison and Bernie Worrell lean over their instruments. We see singers Edna Holt and Lynn Mabry below, on Byrne's right, eerily illuminated by white spotlights, their torsos bent painfully far backwards as Byrne's had been a moment before. Very slowly and gracefully, Holt and Mabry raise themselves upright. Meanwhile, Byrne chants, 'time isn't holding us; time isn't after us', leaning into the microphone, which he now holds in his left hand, while keeping his right arm raised, palm out, implying a blessing or the imminent laying on of hands. Byrne's repetitive invocation ends in incoherent babbling that brings to mind the charismatic practice of 'speaking in tongues'. His words appear magically to cause the two singers' bodies to rise. The audience bears witness to a 'miracle' in which the faux evangelist has 'resurrected' Holt and Mabry.

In the music video, Byrne only takes his 'evangelical send-up' so far (Turim 2007: 103). In the concert film, he has at his disposal the technological resources of the rock concert and the cinema. In the video, Byrne performs alone for the camera; in Demme's film, he commands a musical ensemble backing him, and draws on the energy of an audience. Maureen Turim detects in the music video Byrne's admiration for the preacher's exuberance. In the segment from *Stop Making Sense*, however, Byrne is not so much a preacher as a missionary proving his power over the two black women beside him. We might say that these back-up singers stand in for the African women who appear in the anthropological film clips Byrne points to in order to designate 'another part of the world' in the 'Once in a Lifetime' music video. Holt and Mabry are raised up not merely through the power of words but through imitating Byrne's bodily movements. In fact, throughout the show, they mimic his awkward and mechanical gestures. One imagines Byrne forcing a rigid ballet on what might have been more fluid movements. In 'Slippery People', Holt and Mabry imitate Byrne's awkward marionette-like movements and his frantic strumming of an invisible guitar. This goofy dance parodies the typical cock-rock posing that has made air guitar – unfortunately – something of a folk art.

Both Hendrix and Byrne sought artistic legitimacy or authenticity from crossing racial boundaries. The difference lay in their reception: the public regarded Hendrix as a proficient instrumentalist, Byrne as a smart conceptualist. Hendrix, trying to forge a place for the black musician in rock music (to be distinguished from 1950's rock & roll), found himself up against the existing racialist discourse that positioned black musicians as entertainers – as *artistes* perhaps – but not as genuine artists. Byrne, who enjoyed the aura of the avant-garde artist, fronted a band that played funk adequately but felt the need not only to *sound* blacker but also *to become visibly blacker*. The generally accepted version of biographical events is that Hendrix's manager Michael Jeffery and the demands of the pop star's largely white audience frustrated his attempts to embrace blackness by working with band mates Buddy Miles, Billy Cox and percussionist Juma Sultan. Thus, Hendrix ended his career fronting a revived Jimi Hendrix Experience. Sadly, Hendrix became a favourite with young white 'heads' but could not attract a significant number of black fans. The successful crossover mix of hard rock and funk/soul would actually arrive with George Clinton's Parliament/Funkadelic. A film such as *Mothership Connection* (1998), which documents a concert from P-Funk's 1976 tour, provides an example of the sort of liberating celebration the band offered audiences. It may be enlightening to contrast the carnival of P-Funk's stage show with the artsy elegance of Talking Heads because P-Funk clearly influenced the latter band not only musically but also visually. The two bands even share personnel in keyboardist Bernie Worrell, who appears in the P-Funk film shirtless and sporting a colourful, oversized floppy hat. P-Funk's outrageous costumes, masks and verbal expositions of bizarre mythology may look similar to performances by those avant-garde jazz musicians associated with the Association for the Advancement of Creative Musicians such as the Art Ensemble of Chicago, or Sun Ra's Arkestra. But a P-Funk concert is more stoned 'party' than ecstatic ritual.

Certain images no doubt strike many spectators as plain silly. For example, guitarist Gary Shider appears on stage wearing a diaper and sucking on a pacifier during his guitar solo.

We have a hard time imagining Byrne moving like Clinton. I do not mean to perpetuate racialist essentialist stereotypes of blacks and whites – to insist, for example, that all blacks can dance and that whites cannot.[11] Rather, I want to raise the question of which gestures appropriately accompany certain music. Although Byrne's jerky dancing synchronises with the music's metric pulse and its rhythmic figures, his movements do not 'fit' what we hear. Instead, Byrne offers a critique of the rock star as masculine virtuoso. However, the tendency to regard Byrne's performance style as art crossing over into pop culture and Hendrix's or Clinton's as rock & roll *kitsch* has much to do with the discourse on race has influenced the reception of American music.

NOTES

1 Anno Mungen notes that the 'lack of any discernable effect on the sound is a crucial part of that virtuosity' (2003: 68). Lawrence Kramer describes the 'vexed relationship between virtuosity and visuality' (2002: 70).

2 Hegel does allow that 'so long as he [i.e., the performer] proceeds with spirit, skill, and grace, he may even interrupt the melody with jokes, caprices, and virtuosity' (1975: 957).

3 As Simon Frith observes, 'There is a long history in Romanticism of defining black culture … as the body, the other of the bourgeois mind' (1996: 127).

4 On this topic, see Theodore Gracyk (1996). See also Philip Auslander's response to Gracyk (1999: 62–4).

5 James Parker praises Hendrix's appropriation of the National Anthem as a 'pop-art masterpiece' (2009: 36). Charles Shaar Murray, author of what is arguably the finest book on Hendrix, calls that performance 'the most complex and powerful work of American art to deal with the Vietnam war' (1989: 24). Steve Waksman describes it as 'stunning political critique' (2001: 172).

6 Antoine Fuqua's *Lightning in a Bottle* (2004) contains a segment showing Hendrix at a Buddy Guy show. The film shows Guy playing guitar on his knees, and features a voice-over in which Guy relates how Hendrix observed him playing the guitar behind his back.

7 However, Baraka goes on to consider the possibility that the 'burlesqued' elements of the performance might be integral to the blues, in that they function to distinguish blues 'from the social implications of the white popular song' (1963: 173).

8 The show featured Hendrix with Billy Cox on bass and Mitch Mitchell on drums.

9 Among his credits, he had done cinematography for David L. Weiss's *No Vietnamese Ever Called Me a Nigger* (1968).

10 Lott calls this attire Gillespie's way of 'signifying on fancy city dress' (1995: 247).

11 On race and rhythm, see Radano's chapter 'Of Bodies and Soul' (2003: 230–77).

DIRECT CINEMA, ROCK AND ROLL'S PUBLIC PERSONA AND THE EMERGENCE OF THE ROCK STAR

P. J. O'Connell's book on Robert Drew (1992) contains an afterward ostensibly designed to allow Drew to correct factual errors and omissions and to respond to O'Connell's interpretation of events. Among this material, particularly noteworthy is the acrimonious exchange – mediated through O'Connell – between Drew and his former colleague D. A. Pennebaker. In the late 1950s and early 1960s, Drew Associates not only invented light-weight portable sync-sound equipment but also pioneered the innovative practice of journalistic reporting that came to be known as *direct cinema* or American *cinéma vérité*, which favoured uncontrolled and unscripted situations, live sound recording and minimal or no voice-over narration. So the story goes, the departure of Pennebaker and Richard Leacock from Drew Associates marked the end of this golden age. Decades after the break-up of the 'dream team', the various parties are still suffering from unhealed wounds, as O'Connell's text shows. My primary reason for invoking this dialogue is to bring to the reader's attention the weird contest in which Drew and Pennebaker accuse one another of promoting performances at the expense of real life. Drew dismisses the charge that he actively sought professional performers as subjects as 'absurd' and insists that, on the contrary, it was he and not Pennebaker who was determined 'to get us out of these stadiums and shows' (quoted in O'Connell 1992: 224). He hurls Pennebaker's accusation back at him: 'if you look at what happened after Pennebaker left Drew Associates … he became more and more dedicated to performances'. Then, Drew delivers the *coup de grace*: 'his [Pennebaker's] films are performance films' (1992: 224). This verbal exchange is almost farcical, as each man tries to outdo the other in denying his fascination with and exploitation of performance. I say farcical because direct cinema's intimate association with public performers of all types – actors and politicians, but especially musicians – has been well documented. Not least among direct cinema's appeal is its way of exploiting the tension between the star's public image and private life (see Waugh 1990: 72–3). Whereas the former is suspected as mere façade, the latter is assumed to be the real McCoy.

Paradoxically, direct cinema represents people whose performing talent accounts for their celebrity as most interesting when doing something other than performing in public. I am struck by the paradox that, amidst the rhetoric of capturing the truth, this truth is to be found off-stage rather than on. Keith Beattie has noted the rockumentary's tendency to treat backstage as 'an area which supposedly offers unmediated glimpses of the "real" person behind the performance' (2008: 62). Jonathan Romney writes that, in our celebrity-obsessed culture, 'backstage' represents 'a world behind the curtain in which the real being, the ineffable precious essence of the performer's self, supposedly lies shielded from sight' (1995: 83). Such beliefs imply a naïveté concerning the performative dimension involved in the construction of the self. Albert Maysles, for example, speaks of *What's Happening!: The Beatles in the U.S.A.* (1964) as a new kind of documentary that provides an intimate look at celebrities (in this case the Beatles) in 'behind the scenes fashion', yet it is hard to tell if the backstage footage reveals anything essential about the celebrities. Despite hopes of glimpsing the genuine person in an unguarded moment, backstage eavesdropping might reveal less about the performers as people than the Maysles and their associates believed or claimed. Such uncritical faith in the transparency of private moments backstage is merely the flip side of the belief in the opacity of public performance. However, performances that announce themselves as such appear to be nothing but surface because we insist on looking behind, inside or under them while relegating the information given to our senses as insignificant. Perhaps the phenomena we observe are not 'thin' in themselves; rather, it is our descriptions of them that need to thicken.[1] Once we resist reducing meaning to the emotional revelations of an authentic, 'true' self – a 'ghost in the machine' as it were – the gestures and actions that performers make on-stage can appear significant. One could even argue that, off-stage, subjects have the presence of mind to construct self-conscious presentations of their 'true' selves, whereas, on-stage, a performer is less likely to adjust his or her behaviour for the camera.[2] A more defensible theory, however, would examine *both* situations as performances.

Direct cinema developed along with the rock and folk music of the 1960s. These movies grabbed the attention of fans of the new music, and many young people developed a taste for documentary as a result of their desire to see their favourite performers 'live' on screen. The subjects' celebrity accounts for the films' extraordinary popularity and no doubt contributed to so many of them obtaining theatrical distribution. As Brian Winston puts it, 'direct cinema made the rock performance/tour movie into the most popular and commercially viable documentary form thus far. These were for many the only sort of documentary they saw and responded to positively' (1995: 205). Certainly, the seemingly sincere, unobtrusive approach of direct cinema was just right for making movies of talented youth for public exhibition. For young viewers eager to abandon the hypocritical conformism of the 1950s, 'the behind the scenes candour (and/or clowning) appeared to be more compelling as evidence than the reconstructed encounters of the classic documentary' (ibid.). Such films not only transformed the public's notion of documentary but also promoted the new music, helping to launch the British Invasion and advancing the cause of album-oriented rock in the later years of the decade. In this chapter, I will show how the nonfiction cinema of the 1960s promoted the music and contributed to the emergence of the rock star. Although I look at several films, I treat those of the Maysles brothers as my primary case studies, and I focus particularly on Mick Jagger in *Gimme Shelter* as the quintessential representative of this type of star performer.

I do not mean to overstate the case for the Maysles' films as catalysts for establishing rock music as the ubiquitous social phenomenon and massive industry it would become in the 1970s. The Beatles' and Stones' television appearances no doubt played a greater promotional role. Then, too, we should consider the impact of Steven Binder's concert movie *The T.A.M.I. Show* (1964). While virtually unknown to the general movie-going public, Binder's film acquired legendary status among aficionados of the new rock music. Also worth mention is the ABC television special *The Beatles at Shea Stadium* (NEMS Enterprises, 1966). Finally, the enormous popularity of Richard Lester's *Hard Day's Night* (1964) easily eclipsed that of any contemporary performance film, including the Maysles' *What's Happening!*. Still, the Maysles' films are important models of the rockumentary genre. As Winston notes, *What's Happening!: The Beatles in the U.S.A.*, along with Pennebaker's *Dont Look Back*, established the rock documentary's form. These films provided prototypes for later *verité* rock docs such as *Madonna: Truth or Dare* (Alek Keshishian and Mark Aldo Miceli, 1991) and *Metallica: Some Kind or Monster* from 2004.[3] Moreover, *Gimme Shelter* represents direct cinema's ability to combine musical entertainment with social commentary.

Albert and David Maysles' *What's Happening!* was the first *verité* documentary about a rock band as well as the first sync-sound documentary without voice-over narration (see Mamber 1974: 146). It was not, however, the first *verité* film on a pop star. That honour belongs to *Lonely Boy* (Wolf Koenig and Roman Kroiter, 1962), a portrait of singer Paul Anka produced by the National Film Board of Canada. The film's narrator promises the spectator 'a candid look at Paul Anka from both sides of the footlights'. Released two years before *What's Happening!*, the film proves that Anka was eliciting hysterical reactions from teenage fans even before the Beatles' arrival in North America. On film, Anka describes the arduous task of changing from a 'fat' kid with unruly hair into a pop idol. To hear Anka tell it, show business success entails a transformation of the body from ordinary to ideal. In one scene, Anka's manager, Irving Feld, presents an inventory of his client's features, praising his eyes and his mouth, and frankly admitting to his client's nose job. The star now looks so handsome, he claims, that people would not recognise him from old pictures. Anka's body has undergone a change so radical that the performer has virtually assumed a new identity. He has cultivated an image that Feld contrasts with other images (i.e. old photographs) rather than with the 'real' Paul Anka.

To spectators bored by the bland style of 'professional' television journalism, the candid look of *Lonely Boy* might make the appearance of such a genuine being seem possible. One scene shows the singer in his dressing room in a frenzied rush to get on stage. It is not illogical to infer that, if Anka is unconcerned to be photographed in his white briefs, he might also forget himself, drop the protective veneer of his celebrity image, and reveal something of the true Paul Anka.

It was around the time of *Lonely Boy*'s broadcast that the original Drew Associates began to fall apart. Pennebaker and Richard Leacock pulled out in 1963. Albert Maysles, also an alumnus, formed his own production company with his brother David in 1962. The Maysles brothers worked as a team, with Albert on camera and David recording sound. David also played the key role in overseeing the cutting, which was done (and still is done) by a few talented editors, including Charlotte Zwerin, who received co-director's credit on *Gimme Shelter*. The Maysles were the first to call their films 'direct cinema', an approach that entailed the filmmaker's non-intervention in events happening before the camera, which were to be recorded according to no previous script or direction of the social actors involved.

No doubt many of the most compelling moments in direct cinema do occur off-stage: Mick Jagger's and Charlie Watts' stunned reaction to the gruesome images of the violence in *Gimme Shelter*, for instance. Nevertheless, as Georgia Bergman, Jagger's personal assistant at the time, notes, for the touring musician the interval between shows is consumed mostly with traveling, eating and doing laundry (2000). Her claim admittedly has a disingenuous ring to it, considering her anecdote about the 'groupie' with a pound of butter in her purse roaming a hotel in search of Mick Jagger. No doubt Keith Richards does not spend his down time eating burgers and sorting laundry; nevertheless, despite claims of 'total access', *Gimme Shelter* exposes no one indulging in kinky sex or hard drugs – just rock & roll.[4] On the basis of what we see in *Gimme Shelter* and *What's Happening!*, the Rolling Stones – those bad boys of rock & roll – appear to behave no worse than the Fab Four on their first US visit.[5]

Joe McElhaney's excellent monograph on Albert Maysles reports five different versions of *What's Happening!*. Along with the original Maysles' cut, the most widely seen version is *The Beatles: The First U.S. Visit* (1991), which was edited by long-time Maysles collaborators Susan Froemke and Kathy Dougherty. Understandably, McElhaney prefers the Maysles' cut over the latter version. Noting that *What's Happening!* 'shows little interest in showcasing the Beatles' musical talents', McElhaney labels *The First U.S. Visit* 'largely a performance film' (2009: 67). According to McElhaney, *What's Happening!* and *Gimme Shelter* 'each contain a sequence that, in condensed form, encapsulates the differences' between the Stones and the Beatles. In *What's Happening!*, he identifies that sequence as the band's visit to the Peppermint Lounge. In *Gimme Shelter*, the segment shows the Stones in the studio recording 'Wild Horses" (2009: 86). In other words, for McElhaney, the concert and television performance footage reveals little about the contrasts between these two groups. I would argue that, on the contrary, it is in the stage material that the differences become manifest: for example, can we imagine the Stones playing a ballad from a Broadway musical ('Till There was You') at Altamont, or those neatly-dressed, fresh-faced mop-tops singing 'Street Fighting Man' on *The Ed Sullivan Show*?

Albert Maysles justifiably complains that on stage the distinct personalities of John, Paul, George and Ringo seem to blur.[6] The matching suits and the precise choreography were, after all, designed to produce an effect of collectivity. For instance, perhaps the practice of three singers sharing two microphones was initially dictated by financial limitations, but by the time the band arrived in the US, the microphones had become props in a complex ballet performed by John, Paul and George. In 'She Loves You', all three front men shake their heads together, drawing attention to their bowl haircuts. In contrast, the Stones retained the sense of five individuals playing music together. This is not to say that the Stones were the more democratic band. Whereas the Beatles had three singer-songwriters in the front line, a hierarchy developed among the members of the Stones. Jagger, whose eccentric dance moves and distinctive facial features set him apart from his band mates, 'fronted' the band as lead singer. Guitarists Brian Jones and Keith Richards stood back a bit, the rhythm section of Charlie Watts and Bill Wyman occupied the rear, and pianist Ian Stewart went either unseen or unnoticed.

In 1969 the departure of guitarist Brian Jones allowed Jagger to become the band's undisputed figurehead, a position he has continued to hold. Although Keith Richards' notoriously decadent lifestyle has earned him mythical status among rock fans, it would be safe to say that Jagger represents the Stones' public face. Amy Taubin has astutely noted that Jagger is 'never as comfortable inside his own skin as when he's performing' (2000: 8), and Keith Beattie declares it fruitless to ask whether the Mick Jagger we see on screen is being genuine or acting since, for the pop star, 'the two conditions coalesce' (2008: 72). In fact, Pennebaker might just as well have been describing the Stones' lead singer when he called Bob Dylan 'a guy acting out his life' (quoted in Hall 1998: 227). The enormous celebrity enjoyed by 1960s pop music stars like Dylan and Jagger must have made considerable demands on these men's emotional and cognitive resources, leaving little in reserve for building a rich private life. The urge to shine a light on that tiny remainder no doubt partially accounts for direct cinema's fascination with unrehearsed incidents that happen in dressing rooms rather than with the show on stage.

The question might arise as to why I have not given equal weight to Pennebaker's documentary on Dylan's 1965 tour of England, *Dont Look Back*. For one thing, in 1965, Dylan had not yet completed the transformation from folk singer to folk rocker. Pennebaker shows Dylan welcomed by adoring crowds in England; groupies congregate outside his hotel window, and journalists hang on his every word. His first electric album, *Bringing it All Back Home*, had been released and was stirring up controversy among fans. Clearly, Dylan possesses the star quality to mark him as special. Nevertheless, although Dylan may be a rocker on vinyl and a rock star off-stage, on-stage he is a folkie performing solo with his guitar and harmonica.

Through sheer longevity the Rolling Stones would eventually claim the title of the 'world's greatest rock & roll band'. Throughout the 1960s, however, the media promoted a rivalry between the Beatles and Stones. One obvious difference between the two bands is the number of members in each. Pop groups in the early 1960s had limited options for choosing instrumentation. Of course, guitars and drums were *de rigueur*; keyboards were optional – the portable organ more common than the piano, which was difficult to amplify, hard to transport and often of poor quality in clubs and halls. The lead singer could also augment the standard two guitars, bass and drums line up. The addition of a front man who contributes nothing to the instrumental sound has serious consequences for a band's economics. That singer must possess considerable talent and appeal to justify splitting the money five ways instead of four. On stage, the lead singer's presence establishes another level of visual hierarchy, with the singer always centre-stage and the guitarists flanking him or her. In the case of the Stones, the visual effect is enhanced by Jagger's distinctive voice. Moreover, Keith Richards' backing vocals usually sound only distantly related to Jagger's lead vocal line. In contrast, during the Beatles' early career especially, Lennon's and McCartney's voices complemented each other to an uncanny degree. Often singing melodies in unison, their matching timbre, accurate pitch and exact phrasing gave the impression of a single voice that had been double tracked. When Harrison joined in, the three voices harmonised sweetly – perhaps too sweetly for a rock & roll band. Even drummer Ringo Starr sang live – an awkward occasion that required placing the microphone to pick up his vocals without amplifying the drums too much. For the most part, however, it was the guitarists who bore the dual task of playing and singing. Consequently, most of the stage action took place around the microphone stands, which were essentially anchored in place. In contrast, unfettered by a guitar hanging around his neck, Jagger was free to grab the microphone and roam the stage. By 1969 he had developed a repertoire of gestures, poses and dance moves influenced by American R&B performers like James Brown. Zwerin recalls the hilarious effect of Jagger's 'bumps and grinds' on her friends who had never seen a Stones' show (*Gimme Shelter* DVD commentary).

There is a tendency to regard *What's Happening!* and *Gimme Shelter* as documents of the beginning and end of the belief in rock music as harbinger of peace, love and community.[7] The significance of these two films as bookends of 1960s counterculture should not be exaggerated, however. Having little direct impact on the social and political affairs of the late 1960s, the first British Invasion's influence was relatively contained within the spheres of pop music and fashion. So much happened in the mere five years between the two films: the rise of FM radio, the advent and spread of psychedelic drugs in society at large, the increasingly violent confrontations between protesters and supporters of the Vietnam War, the Robert Kennedy and Martin Luther King assassinations, the conflict between police and the Black Panthers, the debacle at the Democratic Chicago Convention in 1968, the demise of SDS and rise of the Weathermen, and so on. The tendency towards violence was reflected in the militant rhetoric of bands like Jefferson Airplane, whose 1969 album *Volunteers* called for outright revolution rather than non-violent protest. Having played all three major rock festivals of the decade – Monterey, Woodstock (although they do not appear in the film) and Altamont – Jefferson Airplane, an American group, might make a better case study than either the Beatles or the Stones. Still, I agree with Robert Wilonsky's suggestion that the two Maysles movies (*What's Happening!* and *Gimme Shelter*) work well as a double feature. Indeed, Albert Maysles admits he never thinks of one without the other (Wilonsky 2004; and see Saunders 2007).

The practice of providing director's commentary on DVD releases of films such as *Gimme Shelter* effectively disproves the claim that *cinéma vérité* has no need for voice-over commentary. To the contrary, the films benefit enormously from the explication of scenes and the identification of key people – underlining the special status of the on-screen image's relation to actual people and events existing outside the film world. Given the opportunities digital technology has made available, David Maysles' death in 1987 represents a significant loss for music fans, film buffs and scholars. Fortunately, his brother has survived, and he and editor Charlotte Zwerin (who passed away in 2004) have provided extensive commentary on the DVD of *Gimme Shelter*. In contrast to these informative discussions, Maysles' commentary on the 2003 DVD release of the Beatles' film is less loquacious and offers little enlightenment. For instance, he has little to say about the images of the Beatles' appearance on *The Ed Sullivan Show*. To an extent, this reticence makes sense since the CBS television crew and not the Maysles brothers took this footage. If Albert Maysles had obtained approval of the final cut, the film would not include the Sullivan material (see Wilonsky 2004). As the band runs through several numbers in slick fashion, Maysles cannot resist throwing out the disclaimer that 'we prefer to shoot the backstage stuff' – which, in this context, sounds a bit like sour grapes. Prevented from filming the Beatles 'live' in the studio, the Maysles instead persuaded a New York City family, chosen at random, to allow themselves to be filmed watching the programme on their living room TV set. Indeed, the Maysles brothers preferred such improvised situations to rehearsed stage performances. It is this ability to adapt – this knack for turning obstacles into opportunities – that accounts for their success in catching the telling 'small detail'. On the DVD commentary, Maysles also seizes the opportunity to tout the superiority of his 'advanced' camera to the bulky TV equipment. The unimposing size of this gear lets Albert sneak his camera into the Beatles' concert at the Washington Coliseum. For this show, the band performed on a stage placed in the auditorium's centre, the audience surrounding them on four sides. To avoid playing with their backs to a portion of the audience for the entire concert, the band was obliged to move their equipment ninety degrees between each number. Albert boasts of capturing a complete take of 'She Loves You', which he shot from his seat at the show, explaining how the variety afforded by the zoom lens offset the constraint of having to shoot the entire song as a single wide shot. Although the Maysles may prefer the backstage stuff, for me the stage performances offer some relief from the Beatles' relentless sophomoric shenanigans we see in the hotels and trains. I believe it is the monotonous silliness of these latter scenes that makes the sequence of the band and friends partying in New York's Peppermint Lounge club so distinctive as well. Here, the music is too loud and the crowd too thick for the Beatles to command the camera's and tape recorder's sole attention. The 'boys' seem too relaxed to bother staying in character. This segment also contains some poignant shots of middle-aged disk jockey Murray the K ('the fifth Beatle') on the dance floor, straining to keep up with these guys half his age. Apart from this scene, however, the Beatles never cease playing to the camera.

GIMME SHELTER

The Maysles brothers initially undertook the project that would become *Gimme Shelter* hoping to offset the financial loss of their previous film, *Salesman* (1969). Although many consider the latter work a masterpiece, the unglamorous Bible salesmen who serve as the film's subjects obviously lack the box-office appeal of rock stars such as the Beatles or Stones. Cinema scholars do not – or should not – base critical judgements on a film's popularity, of course. In fact, Stephen Mamber considers *Gimme Shelter* less interesting than the Maysles' earlier films, even though he pronounces it 'the most widely seen and discussed' of the brothers' works; Mamber complains that 'a large part of the film is *simply* records of performances' (1974: 172; my emphasis). I imagine that Mamber would hesitate to call a recording 'simple' if he were speaking of something other than a pop music performance. It appears that legitimacy or value depends on the importance of the profilmic material and not on the creative treatment of that material in a specific medium. If it's what happens in front of the camera that counts, the goings on of pop music concerts rank low as the subject of serious documentaries.

Still, Mamber has a point. The concert and studio footage obfuscates the film's suspenseful plot. For viewers who care to look beyond the musicians' charisma, Zwerin has constructed a tragedy set to a rock & roll soundtrack. The concert promoters' hubris is evident, for example, in their blind optimism – believing they could successfully move the concert from Golden Gate Park to the Altamont Speedway at the last minute. The film, however, takes care to blame not only the counterculture's naiveté but also those predators – sleazy entrepreneurs as well as outlaw bikers – skulking around the hippie movement. One particularly telling moment occurs in attorney Melvyn Belli's office, in a scene that exposes speedway owner Dick Carter as a reckless opportunist. Following a terse telephone exchange between Belli, Carter and the highway patrol over inadequate parking at the site, the camera lingers on Belli's face during an uncharacteristically silent pause that suggests the inadequate planning leading up to the event.

Mamber's attitude toward the performance footage does not imply that musical performances are transparent but, rather, that they are opaque. What you see is all you get. In general, commentary on the killing of Meredith Hunter raises questions concerning the victim's state of mind. Did he intend to shoot Jagger or someone else on stage? The intent of Hunter's killer is also relevant. Did the Hell's Angel who stabbed Hunter feel threatened? In contrast, performers are treated as zombies; no insight into their psychology is necessary for analysing how they perform on stage. Of course, no one actually believes performers are zombies; nevertheless, the body/mind split persists in our discourse. Musical performances draw on extensive training and rehearsal, yet we describe dull, routine performances as lacking in spirit. At Altamont, Jagger certainly appears to be going through the motions mechanically. But how can the musicians apply their minds to their music with so many disruptions? No doubt Jagger was stunned by violence he had not anticipated. Daniel Schowalter, who has analysed conservative jeremiads against rock festivals and rock music, reports how critics claim that, under the music's power, musicians and fans 'lose their sense of agency' and are rendered incapable of organised collective action; these attacks on rock's corrupting influence assert that by the time the Maysles shot *Gimme Shelter*, the hippie masses were ready for 'mindless, frenetic violence' (2000: 95). The reference to 'mindless' violence implies that the audience members, as well as performers, are zombies.

How can what happens on stage compare with the bodies beaten during the concert; one body, that of Meredith Hunter, fatally stabbed; and another body, that of Alan Passaro, the Angel who wielded the knife, arrested for murder?[8] After Hunter's death the Stones finished their set without major incident. This return to business as usual caused some critics to wonder how the band could callously go on playing. If not implicated in the murder, the Stones seem guilty of gross insensitivity. In the festival's aftermath rumours circulated: (1) Jagger's announcing the concert – the Stones' appearance was supposed to be a surprise – was calculated to guarantee a large crowd for the film; (2) the Stones delayed taking the stage until after dark so the stage lights would have the right effect. Other critics offer alibis: 'Accustomed to disorder and hysteria in their audiences, the Rolling Stones continued their concert, pathetically unaware that the "fracas" up front was not a run-of-the-mill "rumble" between gangs or an ordinary free-for-all fight' (Issari & Paul 1979: 131).

SOMETHING VERY FUNNY HAPPENS WHEN WE START THAT NUMBER

Rumours claim the murder happened during 'Sympathy for the Devil' whereas, actually, it occurred during 'Under My Thumb', a fact that Jonathan Vogels makes much of in pointing out the irony that pandemonium breaks out 'while Jagger sings of regaining control within a relationship'. Keith Beattie identifies 'Sympathy for the Devil' as 'the song which the Stones attempt to perform as the fan, Meredith Hunter, is murdered by Hell's Angels' (2008: 71). My aim is not to chide Beattie for his research. After all, no reliable explanatory narrative of events has emerged over the past forty years. Even the visible evidence showing the stabbing has failed to establish unambiguously the cause of death for Hunter, whose murder was officially declared unsolved in 2005. Of course, no one has admitted hiring the Hell's Angels to perform any sort of security function. Albert Maysles has revealed that more footage of the Altamont event exists, and this revelation has produced calls for the release of these outtakes as a bonus feature on future DVDs. Such a concession to morbid curiosity is not likely to happen, since the Maysles have had to refute charges of sensationalism from critics such as Vincent Canby and Pauline Kael (see Ellis & McLane 2005; McElhaney 2009). The existence of this extra footage holds out the promise of truth, but only as long as the footage stays in the vaults. The unused footage shot at Altamont would most likely yield no new revelations about the killing. No narrative adequately explains it: as much becomes clear from watching and listening to the extensive 'extras' already available on the Criterion DVD. These include a broadcast from radio station KSAN that contains testimony from Stones' road manager Sam Cutler, a Hell's Angel known as 'Pete from San Francisco', Sonny Barger and others. Extensive galleries of still photos taken by Bill Owens and Beth Sunflower provide additional visual material. What emerges from this supplementary audio-visual information is a confused picture of a complex and over-determined situation.

Perhaps more crucial than sorting out all the facts is noticing how Zwerin sacrifices chronological accuracy for dramatic effect. Her skill as an editor renders the cut between the end of 'Under My Thumb' and the deadly scuffle virtually seamless. Yet, according to the 'eyewitness' testimony of Stanley Booth, Sonny Barger and others, Hunter was attacked at the very beginning of 'Under My Thumb' and not immediately after the song had ended. Given this information, the attack could not have occurred after Jagger's final line, 'I pray that it's alright', as Vogels claims (2005: 92). As he sings this line, a subdued Jagger hangs on the microphone stand – quite a contrast with the manic entertainer who belts out 'Jumpin' Jack Flash' in the film's beginning. Anyone who has performed before an audience can attest to the latter's impact on the music. In a previous chapter, we saw how many non-Western cultures do not limit a musical event to sonic effects nor maintain a radical separation between those who produce sounds on instruments and other participants. In Western art music, John Cage, especially through his composition *4'33"*, attempted to deconstruct the boundaries between sonic events happening on stage, which are deemed musical, and events occurring in the audience, which are dismissed as noise. In this spirit, the Altamont concert should be regarded as a totality rather than as two discrete historical occurrences: a music festival *and* a violent clash between the counterculture and an outlaw biker club. On that day, the Angels' violent behaviour affected Jagger's performance and we can note that effect on film. The interruptions that frustrate the Stones' attempts to finish certain numbers have become part of the experience of *Gimme Shelter*.

The question of which song Jagger was singing at the moment of Hunter's murder nevertheless retains some significance. During Hunter's murder was Jagger voicing words attributed to an unremarkable misogynistic male or to the veritable prince of darkness? Following Simon Frith (1996), Philip Auslander proposes a thicker analysis of how performers operate. Auslander (2006) regards the performer's persona as comprised of three layers: as actual human being, as self-presentation and as character in the song text. As front man, Jagger draws on both his physical presence and his presentational 'image'; as singer, he assumes the role of protagonist of the song text.

Hell's Angel Sonny Barger claims that the Stones 'got exactly what they originally wanted – a dark, scary environment to play 'Sympathy for the Devil'' (Barger 2001: 166). Shawn Levy calls 'Sympathy for the Devil' 'the song that would define them separately from the Beatles forever' (2005: 26). However, as already pointed out, the Stones had always projected a darker, more dangerous image than their rivals. The climax of *Gimme Shelter* is not the performance of a song but the death of a concertgoer.

Yet, as McElhaney astutely observes, the film is 'fundamentally uninterested in finding a clear meaning in relation to the murder'. Instead, he notes, it appears fascinated with 'the charisma and physicality of the Stones (especially Jagger) and the kind of spectacle that this engenders' (2009: 77). This comment lends support to my claim that one of the most prominent differences between the Beatles and the Stones is how Jagger comes to stand apart from the rest of the band. McElhaney singles out the performance of 'Jumpin' Jack Flash' at Madison Square Garden as 'a star moment for Jagger' (2009: 78). I want to dwell on that moment and then examine Brian Jones' departure and subsequent death, which left Jagger the figurehead and *de facto* leader of the group. As Jones' replacement, the Stones hired Mick Taylor, whose self-effacing stage manner posed no challenge to Jagger's domination of the stage. In the New York shows, Maysles fixes the camera on Jagger during 'Jumpin' Jack Flash', clearly affirming the singer's role as the band's front man. Armed with a single camera and sitting on soundman Stan Goldstein's shoulders, Maysles shoots from an angle that shows Jagger flanked by a sedate Taylor, standing nearly motionless, concentrating on playing his guitar. When Jagger dances across the stage, the camera follows, and it remains on Jagger even during Taylor's brief but well-played guitar solo. A similar elision of Taylor occurs during 'Satisfaction' as well. Of course, such attention paid to Jagger was hardly unique. For instance, during the performance of 'It's All Over Now' in *The T.A.M.I. Show*, the camera operator appears unable to determine where to train the lens. During the vocal sections, Jagger understandably provides the focus. However, during the guitar solo, the camera briefly seeks out Jones only to switch quickly back to Jagger, whose frenetic dancing is clearly upstaging his mates – including Keith Richards, who is actually playing the solo.

In contrast to Taylor's anonymity, Brian Jones considerably influenced the band's look despite his quiet demeanour. In fact, many fans preferred his cool attitude to Jagger's manic theatrics. In the 1968 TV special *The Rolling Stones' Rock 'n' Roll Circus* (directed by Michael Lindsay-Hogg, who also directed the Beatles' *Let it Be* (1970)), the band plays a set that includes both 'Jumpin' Jack Flash' and 'Sympathy for the Devil'. These songs sound much closer to the recorded versions than they do on the American tour the following year. On stage, drums and guitars are behind Jagger, who has access to a runway that juts out from the stage. Toward the end of 'Sympathy for the Devil', he dances to the runway's end, falls down on his knees and removes his shirt to reveal tattoos representing the devil on both arms and on his chest. This is Jagger's showcase as well as Jones' farewell performance with the band. Although Jones' slide guitar is featured in 'No Expectations', in 'Sympathy for the Devil' he is reduced to playing maracas. This would be Jones' last public performance; in July 1969 he was found dead in his swimming pool.

More evidence of Jones' estrangement from the band appears in Jean-Luc Godard's film *One Plus One or Sympathy for the Devil* (1968). For this project, Godard films the Stones in the studio, building 'Sympathy for the Devil' by experimenting with rhythmic variations and different instrumentation on top of the song's basic chord structure. The studio *mise-en-scène* emphasises Jones' isolation from the others, as he sits surrounded by sound baffles, strumming an unheard acoustic guitar. As the instrumentation of 'Sympathy for the Devil' becomes increasingly electric, Jones' silent strumming becomes increasingly insignificant and bathetic. One shot shows him clearly lagging behind the chord changes, connoting his marginal contribution to the 'Beggar's Banquet' LP and his waning status as a member of the Rolling Stones.

SOME KIND OF MONSTER

I want to leap ahead to discuss briefly a work by two documentary filmmakers who trained under the Maysles' tutelage and who, in many ways, bear the torch of direct cinema. In the present study, Joe Berlinger's and Bruce Sinofsky's *Metallica: Some Kind of Monster* represents the furthest point from a musical performance film. Not only does it feature minimal concert footage, but also, unlike Godard's film, it does not attempt to chronicle the music's evolution in the recording studio. Instead, it centres on the band's group therapy sessions with psychotherapist Phil Towle. Such a focus on the extra-musical is in line with Berlinger's belief that films about music are 'interesting but not transcendent'. In stronger terms, Sinofsky has dismissed 'concert-driven films' as 'a dime a dozen' (quoted in Anon. 2004). Sinofsky voices his disappointment with *Let it Be*'s focus on musical performance; he confesses his desire 'to see John and Paul and George really expressing what they were feeling about each other, the things that were eating away inside them, and forcing them to break apart' (ibid.). The film is guilty of disregarding the important stuff happening 'inside' the Beatles and focusing instead on their superficial performances. In *Metallica: Some Kind of Monster*, the dramatic wrestling with psychological demons reveals the gentle soul behind the headbanger façade. The emphasis is on character and story. Despite Sinofsky's talk of breaking with the *vérité* tradition, however, the narrative arc conforms to the crisis structure that characterises direct cinema. Will lead singer James Hetfield return to the band after rehab? Will the band finish the record and continue? The plot revolves around this modern-day Odysseus' departure, his hiatus during rehabilitation for alcoholism and his triumphant homecoming.

Like the Stones, Metallica are haunted by the death of a founding member, bassist Cliff Burton. The recent departure of his replacement, Jason Newsted, fails to generate suspense in the film, probably because it pales in comparison to Hetfield's meltdown. *New York Times* critic A. O. Scott cites the search for a new bassist as an example of the film's 'retreat[ing] a little into backstage business as usual' (2004: 10). I would object that, on the contrary, the auditions for a bass player constitute some of the most exciting footage in the film. The montage sequence of various musicians auditioning for the band suggests how well the filmmakers honed their craft while working with Zwerin at Maysles Brothers. Much of these scenes' visual impact derives from bassist Robert Trujillo's charismatic presence and instrumental virtuosity. Less thrilling perhaps, but more touching, are the scenes from Band Appreciation Day that show a young female fan outplaying the male competition and jamming with the band. Her joyful performance – evident in her wide grin – alternates with footage featuring a grim soul-searching exchange between Hetfield and drummer Lars Ulrich. Berlinger and Sinofsky have indeed delivered more than a concert movie, but the film relies too heavily on the gimmick of macho rock stars Hetfield and Ulrich doing couples counselling.

To conclude, I suggest that performances function as part of the rigorously reflexive trial to which nonfiction filmmakers constantly subject their work. In this chapter, I have attempted to examine the films themselves alongside the rhetoric by those filmmakers associated with direct cinema phenomenon. What we get is a portrait of filmmakers obsessed with the nagging fear that in making films about performers they were capturing performances rather than real life. Such a distinction, however, seems untenable in light of the vast amount of theoretical work on notions of the authentic self. On-stage performances can reveal much about music-making as a collaborative endeavour and can help us understand the historical moment when the individual star musician emerged from the collective group.

NOTES

1 Here, I refer to Gilbert Ryle's terminology, which was later adopted by Clifford Geertz. On the differences between 'thin' and 'thick' descriptions see Ryle 1949 and 1971.

2 As both Bill Nichols (2001: 114) and Michael Chanan suggest (2007: 223), in such moments. the exigent demands of 'live' performance take precedence over the filming.

3 Mark Kermode writes of Keshishian and Miceli's Madonna film that 'the antics of today's media-savvy entertainers "caught on camera" backstage are as much of a performance as their onstage routines – it is the appearance, rather than the reality, of intimacy that has latterly replaced the insights of Don't Look Back [sic] and Gimme Shelter' (2006: 81). Such a position implies that Dylan and Jagger were less adept than Madonna at maintaining their personae on camera. I think the evidence of the films and of the criticism suggests otherwise. Moreover, Kermode subscribes to the myth of authenticity that many critics of direct cinema, myself included, put into question.

4 Except, perhaps, Madonna, although her performance of 'Like a Virgin' in Truth or Dare is easily as titillating as – if not more than – her bedroom escapades later in the film.

5 Robert Frank's Cocksucker Blues (1972) supposedly contains all the raw material that Gimme Shelter leaves out. The Stones must have considered it a bit too candid; they prevented the film's distribution.

6 The Beatles' individuality tended to blur off-stage as well. McElhaney points out that 'Like Salesman, What's Happening! follows four men in business suits (and, to the eyes of some at the time, the Beatles were physically interchangeable) as they peddle their wares to a primarily female clientele while spending much of their free time sitting around in hotel rooms' (2009: 71)

7 Of course, the more common contrast is between Gimme Shelter and Wadleigh's Woodstock. But see Saunders 2007.

8 Note that the knife was never inconclusively identified as the murder weapon. The film shows Passaro stabbing Hunter twice; the victim's body, however, had at least six stab wounds and he had been kicked viciously. Passaro's lawyer made much of this fact to argue for reasonable doubt.

INSTRUMENTAL TECHNIQUE AND FACIAL EXPRESSION ON SCREEN

In the cinema, the capacity for non-diegetic music to enrich the picture – to 'add value' to the visual image as Michel Chion (1994) puts it – has long been acknowledged, yet musical performance on screen has difficulty representing something other than performance itself. We might even say that the physical demands of making music actually impoverish the body as sign, anchoring it to a single referential meaning. What, after all, is a concert film about other than the musicians playing their instruments? The performing musician's incompliant body troubles the filmmaker, who, striving to communicate with physical gestures meaningful only to connoisseurs (i.e. those with specialised musical knowledge), searches for alternative images to relay emotions via a code common both to musicians and non-musicians.

Unfortunately, at least according to Siegfried Kracauer, attempts to render musical performance in cinematic ways rarely succeed. For example, instead of adding vitality to the footage, camera movement merely provides distraction. Charged with presenting the performance as spectacle, the cinematographer wanders about seeking variety: 'As if determined to ignore the performance as a musical event, the camera moves along the rows of the brasses and violoncellos, now singles out the soloist or conductor for closer inspection' (1960: 151). Alternatively, the camera 'deserts the orchestra altogether and settles on the enraptured features of a woman in the audience', an idle indulgence Kracauer describes as resembling 'a boy playing truant' (ibid.). I find it interesting that

Kracauer has constructed a dilemma in which the camera either studies the musicians too intently or too desultorily. In this chapter, I want to examine these two practices – this 'closer inspection' and this 'truancy' – for together they constitute the primary strategy for meliorating the tedium that seems to plague the genre of the musical performance documentary. The camera searches for signs of interiority through close-ups of the performer's face or, alternatively, it roams through the audience to find visual material to supplement the music we hear.[1]

I have chosen to concentrate on documentaries featuring famous violinists because the problems these movies collectively pose make for a particularly apposite case study. Of traditional Western orchestral instruments, the violin, played under the performer's chin, offers many opportunities for close-ups that capture both manual technique and facial expression.[2] Thus, it becomes easy to exclude the body from the frame. Consider, for the sake of contrast, the guitar, which hangs at the player's hips. The contoured design of a solid-body electric guitar such as Fender's Stratocaster make it easy to 'hump' the instrument as Jimi Hendrix does in *Monterey Pop*. As noted in chapter two, Hendrix's sexually suggestive moves with his guitar were perceived as signifying base sexual impulses rather than refined emotions.[3] In contrast, violin technique draws the camera towards the body's superior parts, thus lending nobility to the instrument.[4] (Nevertheless, we should not forget that, in spite of its lofty place in the repertoire of the symphony orchestra, the violin is an instrument associated with nomadic peoples such as Jews and gypsies.)

As Kristin Thomson (1985) points out, the actual practice of continuity editing reflects the virtual coherence of the story. That is, the continuity style is intimately bound to the cause-and-effect logic that drives the narratives of fiction film. It is not, of course, the only way to cut a film: art movies, avant-garde films, and documentaries all employ other editing strategies to varying degrees. Bill Nichols notes that documentary editing practice appears discontinuous but actually conforms to a different paradigm. What Nichols calls *evidentiary* cutting 'organises cuts within a scene to present the impression of a single, convincing argument supported by a logic' (2001: 30). This claim is in line with Nichols' distinction between fiction and nonfiction film in which argument replaces story for the latter. In general, analytical editing involves breaking down a scene according to a particular kind of logic. In contrast, in the musical performance film, the motivation for cutting seems to be variation for its own sake. At least, such is Kracauer's complaint.

As already noted, Kracauer considers musical performance *qua* performance inconsistent with the medium of cinema because this type of 'canned' performance (like an opera or a ballet) does not form part of physical reality. Kracauer does not object to performance *per se*, of course, but performance must be representational rather than presentational. Trying to avoid the latter, certain concert films attempt to integrate music into 'cinema reality'. As an example, Kracauer cites *Of Men and Music* (Irving Reis and Alexander Hammid, 1951). This documentary, which features segments on Arthur Rubenstein and Jascha Heifetz among others, consists not only of performance footage but of corny and stagy behind-the-scenes material. These Kracauer finds objectionable: 'not content with simply conveying their performances – which is what it has been produced for after all – it [the film] also affords glimpses of their private existence' (1960: 150). Because the study of musicians as musicians provides the film's *raison d'être*, Kracauer dismisses the non-performance footage as window dressing. Critic Bosley Crowther agrees that these 'naïve and banal stratagems … fail to provide dramatic impulse' (1951). Expressing an attitude quite the opposite of the tendency I have been criticising in this text, Crowther notes: 'If the greatness of these artists as people is supposedly displayed by the stuffy acts they are asked to put on in this picture, then that side of them had better be left alone' (ibid.).

The film features a voice-over narration by Deems Taylor that portrays the renowned virtuoso as an ordinary citizen who understands that 'technique without living is sterile'. Introducing a segment on Heifetz's quotidian home life, the narration emphasises his all-American, masculine interests and hobbies: 'He sails boats, plays tennis and ping-pong with his family and friends, works in his garden, tinkers with gadgets.' The screen then offers a series of close-ups of hands doing these very things: changing a tire, planting flowers. This portrait of the everyday gives way to the story of how Heifetz prepares for a concert tour. The easygoing family man transforms into a serious professional who begins 'a training regime that would shame an athlete'. Heifetz eases into his practice schedule slowly, we are informed, 'as a baseball pitcher would begin slow in the spring'. The effect of this rigorous regime will make the violinist 'as fit as a prize fighter'. It makes sense that, during that conservative epoch in US history when any perceived threat of *otherness* could produce a reactionary panic, the master instrumentalist should be portrayed not as a frail aesthete but as a robust, albeit gifted, artisan. We see Heifetz in his studio intently perusing the score of a well-rehearsed piece of music, always vigilant against the 'constant danger of playing automatically'. The scene underscores how an American retains a sense of individual agency while pursuing his or her vocation.

These pictures of mundane living and rigorous practice lead up to ten minutes of concert footage of Heifetz and his accompanist, pianist Emanuel Bay. This shift is accomplished through a clever transition that highlights cinema's power to reveal what the naked eye cannot see. A segment shows a close-up of Heifetz's hands moving in slow motion. When movement returns to normal, the narrator tells us that 'this is the way the concert audience sees it'. This statement is misleading, however, because the concert audience cannot approach the performer to see as close-up as the camera lens allows. This shot illustrates the kind of phenomena – which Kracauer lists under the rubric of 'transient' movement – that the cinema can reveal to us. Kracauer describes such shots as 'temporal close-ups achieving in time what the close-up proper is achieving in space' (1960: 53).[5] As if to avert our fascination with the superficiality of the merely visible, the narrator reminds us that to comprehend the 'heart' of the musical line, we can only listen. This statement leads from the slow-motion footage to the performance of Wieniaski's *Scherzo Tarantella*.

The performance footage that follows draws on a tiny repertoire of framings mostly rendered as long takes. These can be classified as follows: (1) A low-angle 'single' of Heifetz from the waist up; (2) A 'two-shot' of Heifetz and Bay showing the violinist from the knees up; (3) A two-shot of Heifetz and Bay, this time with both men full figure; (4) A 'bust shot' of Heifetz's right profile, with the violin body and neck clearly visible beyond his face; (5) A long shot of the stage taken from the hall, about eight rows back; (6) An extreme close-up of the violin neck. Framing number (1) shows up five times, claiming about four minutes and twenty-nine seconds total screen time. The ratio of appearance to screen time suggests that most of these are long takes: two of these shots, for instance, last 92 and 83 seconds each. Consider how the preceding inventory of framings resembles the factors that Noël Burch identifies as contributing to the flatness of 'primitive' film's *mise-en-scène*: relatively even illumination, fixed camera, horizontal and frontal placement of camera, the staging of actors as a tableau (1990: 164). Given this overall theatrical approach to the performance, close-ups and cutaways represent the director's attempt to escape the presentational style of early cinema.

I want to turn to a short documentary featuring Heifetz made during the same period, *Meet the Masters: Jascha Heifetz* (1953). Filmed at Claremont College, the film begins with idyllic scenes of campus. We see several shots of two well-dressed men later identified as Heifetz and Bay who are apparently leaving campus after conducting library research. They delay their departure, however, after a Claremont professor persuades them to accompany him to the recital hall and meet with his students. This impromptu colloquium turns into a concert over twenty minutes long.

The performance footage is preceded by three questions from the audience. First, a young woman poses a routine question concerning the master violinist's opinion on 'the most important attributes for a young artist'. Heifetz proffers an equally banal answer: 'self respect … integrity, and enthusiasm'. Next, a second young woman asks him what he thinks about pop music, to which he responds that he likes 'some of it very much'. The third question comes from a young woman obviously stereotyped as an intellectual, who poses a wordy inquiry: 'I know there's a lot of argument about the extent to which, and the method whereby, a musician can vary the tonal quality of an instrument by what we call "touch", but don't you agree that some degree of variation in the immutables of sound is indisputable'? Cut to Heifetz, who hesitantly begins to stammer a reply. Before he can answer, however, the persistent young woman continues, 'Do you see the growth of modern music, that is, beginning with the contrapuntal severity of Bach, coming up to and including the atonality of Schoenberg, as a complete defeat of the necessity of tonality and harmony – or don't you?' Cut back to Heifetz, who pauses stone-faced before finally responding by offering to play for the students. Again we witness an attempt to portray Heifetz as practicing musician rather than reflexive intellectual. It is, of course, absurd that a performer of Heifetz's stature would not have an opinion on modern music. This scene represents a typical dilemma of 1950s America: too little reflection casts the performer as a zombie, too much as an egghead.

Although this film contains twice as much concert footage as *Of Men and Music*, the range of framings offers no greater variety. The Claremont film does make more of a reverse angle reaction shot in which the camera position changes 180 degrees to shoot from the stage into the hall. The most common of these shots shows the audience applauding and does little to alleviate the repetitive framing. More successful is a cutaway to a bust shot of a young couple in the audience, both staring in blissful attention at the performers. Instead of returning us to the stage, the film then cuts to a tighter close-up of a young woman. Rendered in shallow focus and centered in the frame, her glowing face is framed by dark hair, her dark eyes and full lips set amid two broad white cheeks, white forehead and prominent chin. Her look provides a perfect example of what Gilles Deleuze calls the *reflexive face* – a concept we will engage more thoroughly below.

Figure 3 – The reflexive face

THE BLOSSOMING OF THE FACE[6]

When a piece of music instructs a musician to play a passage *con passione*, such commands refer not to the musician's private emotional state but to publicly observable behaviour. Whether or not the player actually *feels* passionate matters little so long as the performance signifies 'passion' for the spectator/ listener. However, for the latter to interpret these words and/or tones (as well as the gestures that accompany them) as particularly passionate rather than, say, plaintive, she must understand the conventions of the performance *code*. We humans are such visually oriented creatures that, when these signs are strictly sonic, they may escape our notice. Furthermore, although the appreciation of music seems virtually universal, musical expertise varies widely among individuals. It takes a trained ear to distinguish between a recording of a professional musician and one of a gifted amateur. Hearing a musical piece of medium difficulty, the average listener may have trouble distinguishing between an Isaac Stern or a Jack Benny. How is it, then, that few spectators would have difficulty distinguishing the musician from the comedian? The fact is that live performers control a listener's interpretive responses through a repertoire of visual cues relayed through bodily gesture, but especially through facial expression. Although Stern and Benny stand worlds apart in their status as musicians, both exploit facial expression in their art. The face is the plastic medium through which a single musical phrase passes in order to move listeners either to laughter or tears.

If much of music's emotional content is conveyed through conventionally meaningful looks produced by the musicians in the concert hall, this strategy applies *a fortiori* in cinema. On this topic, it is worth quoting Bela Belázs at length on this subject:

> The face of a man listening to music ... may throw light into the human soul; it may also throw light on the music itself and suggest by means of the listener's facial expression some experience touched off by this musical effect. If the director shows us a close-up of the conductor while an invisible orchestra is playing, not only can the character of the music be made clear by the dumbshow of the conductor, his facial expression may also give an interpretation of the sounds and convey it to us. And the emotion produced in a human being by music and demonstrated by a close-up of a face can enhance the power of a piece of music in our eyes far more than any added decibels. (1970: 209)

Belázs is claiming that the close-up of the face can communicate the emotional power of music more efficiently than sound itself (at least to the degree that sound is measured in volume). Close-ups of the performer's face lend meaning to inarticulate sound, but racial and cultural differences undermine any claim to facial expression as a sort of universal communicative medium.

DISCIPLINING BODIES

Whereas the visible exertions of the performer's *body* are often treated as a distraction from the music proper, research suggests that audiences respond positively to facial expression, regarding it as the disclosure of genuine feeling as opposed to the display of mere technique.[7] The performer's physical restraint is treated as representing a refinement of emotion that comes with maturity. For instance, as a youthful prodigy, Franz Lizst was known for his flamboyant histrionics on stage; however, as the pianist matured, he restrained his more outrageous gestures and shifted expressivity to his face (see Kramer 2002). These grimaces became the source of the stock facial repertoire of later generations of performers. The presentation of so-called classical music in performance evolved as follows: as signs of emotion became manifest on the brow, the mouth and the eyes, extravagant bodily gestures were tamed, and the face emerged as the primary signifying medium while the available range of bodily signs diminished.

The previous summary could also describe the history of dramatic performance in narrative cinema, telling the now-familiar story of how, as the camera moved closer to the actors, subtle facial expressions increasingly replaced the grand gestures associated with stage acting (see Naremore 1988 and Bowser 1990). The story relates a shift from what Roberta Pearson (1992) identifies as the *histrionic* code to the *verisimilar* code. In essence, actors abandoned overt theatricality for naturalistic effects. The standard history tells of D. W. Griffith's refinement of the close-up and the ascendancy of the movie star, who became recognisable as a *face* – Garbo's, for instance, which, long after the actress had retired from public life, still inspired Roland Barthes to praise its sculpted quality, the thick, white make-up, and the dark eyes, 'two faintly tremulous wounds' (1972: 56). When television arrived, so the story goes, the camera moved even closer to compensate for the smaller screen. In more recent times, the actor's body has further disappeared in what David Bordwell calls the 'stand and deliver' style of acting (2005: 22), which is characterised by frequent cutting and restless camera movement. With bodily gestures restrained, the director usually resorts to the close-up to communicate emotion.[8]

Gilles Deleuze and Felix Guattari in *A Thousand Plateaus* identify the face as the material support for the signifier – the place where signifying occurs and interpretation is prompted (1987: 115).[9] Language (and not just verbal language) speaks through the face, which releases the sign to take its 'line of flight' toward limitless semiosis, but beckons the sign back home as it nears that limit. The neologism *faciality* refers to a system consisting of a flat white surface (a screen) on which signs are inscribed or projected and a black hole that facilitates subject formation. In the cinema, the authors claim, the close-up exploits the face as a landscape full of holes (the mouth, the eyes) (1987: 172). The living being becomes organised through the face, which conquers the head, separates that head from the rest of the body, and makes both disappear. According to Deleuze and Guattari, the face subdues living beings and disciplines bodies. Adult human subjects cast off animal and childlike traits: 'a child who runs around, plays, dances and draws cannot concentrate on language and writing, and will never be a good subject' (1987: 180). To tame unruly, noisy pupils, a sedentary model of traditional musical education in the West has emerged, which trains performers to obey the score's instructions and to conform their bodily gestures to the authoritarian rule of the conductor or choirmaster. A wonderful example of this pedagogy appears in the Hollywood musical *They Shall Have Music* (Archie Mayo, 1939) in which the music teacher chides his pupil: 'If you want people to listen, don't make funny faces.'

The eccentric virtuoso occasionally upsets the chain of command through ostentatious, distracting displays of physical skill. Consider the following contemporary description of Nicolo Paganini, which dwells on the spectacle of his body and its contrast with his vacant face:

> No one was ever so incredibly lean as Paganini; with this, he has a pale complexion, a sharp prominent nose like an eagle's beak and long bony fingers. He seems too frail to bear the weight of his clothes. When he bows to the audience, his movements are so strange that one dreads lest his feet should detach themselves from his body and the whole man disintegrate and crumble to a heap of bones. When he plays, his right foot comes forward, and in the quick rhythms beats time with a vivacity that is almost comical. His face, however, never loses its death-like impassiveness. (Saussine 1954: 106)

The above description says nothing of Paganini's erotic magnetism, an example of which can be seen in the sensational portrait of the sexual and musical virtuoso in *The Red Violin*. In one scene, the star musician's pre-concert sexual escapade has delayed his arrival onstage. When he finally appears, instead of penitence he expresses haughty disdain. Angered by the soloist's insubordination, the conductor throws down his baton and walks away. Once the violinist begins to play, his body launches into exaggerated convulsions. Although this scene, like many others in the film, appears unduly histrionic, it is considerably less so than the one that opens Klaus Kinski's 1989 biopic of the demonic musical genius. Kinski depicts an animalistic Paganini, whose rather grotesque countenance is practically obscured by long, scraggly, black hair. Such depictions fairly abuse the license allowed fiction; still, they give us a visual analogue of Paganini's ferocity and charisma as relayed to us by verbal accounts like the above. Since those times, however, the concert-going public for 'serious' music has lost its taste for such extravagant spectacle. Today's performers must learn to control their bodies and cultivate dignified but evocative facial signals.

We can note the prevalence of the face in many pop music documentaries, as the camera is drawn to the singer's open mouth and the instrumentalist's expressive eyes. For *Dont Look Back*, the new, portable sync-sound equipment allowed Pennebaker to lie on the stage floor in front of Bob Dylan to capture his singing 'The Lonesome Death of Hattie Carroll'.[10] From his supine position, Pennebaker shoots the entire song – as much as he can get before he runs out of film – as a close-up of Dylan's face. Obscured partially by the microphone and Dylan's harmonica holder, that face, with its Semitic features, is young, angelic and inexpressive. Dylan's deadpan delivery downplays sentimentality and emphasises the gravity of the song's subject: the fatal beating of a black maid for serving her master's guests' drinks too slowly. Later in this chapter, I look at another Jewish performer, Jack Benny, whose deadpan style produces a silly rather than a solemn effect. This is the lesson learned from Kuleshov's famous experiment: as a signifying medium, the performer's face relays little information until it is placed in context. Replace the somber words of Dylan's song with ridiculous lyrics and the performer's straight face has another effect on the audience – Bob Dylan becomes a hip Jewish version of Tommy Smothers.

The restrained performances characteristic of 'folk singers' like Dylan contrast with the primitive sexuality of rock & roll singers such as Elvis Presley, whose sneer caused far less of an uproar than his swiveling hips. When Presley first appeared on *The Ed Sullivan Show* in 1956, cameramen were instructed to photograph the singer from the waist up only. Whatever was gained in hiding Presley's gyrating hips and quivering legs emerged in the singer's heavy-lidded eyes and sensuous mouth. The neglect of gesture and the obsession with the look intensifies in the age of the movies and television. The ideal concert hall is built to render the performer's full figure easily viewable from the most distant seat in the house. In the cinema, the close-up allows – or, rather, compels – the audience to scrutinise the face.

If acting in the cinema has come to privilege the face as the location where expression occurs, this holds true especially of Method acting, the most influential school of the last half of the twentieth century.[11] According to the Method's tenets, a successful performance depends on the ability to recall powerful emotions and not on the acquisition of a vast repertoire of bodily poses.[12] Crude versions of the Method have vitiated the histrionic code as routine dumbshow easily distinguished from expressions of genuine feeling. The Method's basic principles are derived from the System set forth by Constantin Stanislavsky, whose teachings were transplanted to the US via his pupil Yevgeny Vakhtangov, took root at Harold Clurman's Group Theater, and flourished at Lee Strasberg's Actors Studio. The success of this approach owes something to Americans' privileging of authenticity over imitation and the individual's search for the 'true self'. According to David Krasner, 'by the time of Stanislavsky's tour of the United States in 1923, the nation was responsive to his ideas of authentic behaviour' (2000: 26). Despite its foreign pedigree, the Stanislavsky school of acting was well suited for 'a culture rooted in individualism and celebrity' like that of the United States (ibid.).

One of the first Stanislavsky-influenced American actors in the cinema was John Garfield (born Jacob Julius Garfinkle), who could lay claim to an urban upbringing and Jewish heritage. In *Humoresque* (Jean Negulesco, 1946), Garfield plays violin virtuoso Paul Boray, whose patron is rich socialite Helen Wright (Joan Crawford). Unlike the typical Hollywood movie that shows the violinist sawing away with the bow while the left hand remains frozen in place, Garfield actually appears to be playing the instrument. However, this is one of cinema's visual tricks. The music we hear was actually played by Isaac Stern, whose fingers are those we see moving along the violin's neck. For such scenes, Garfield stood with his hands behind his back, violin under his chin, with Stern standing behind him on the left while another violinist positioned on his right worked the bow. In the scene after Paul quits his brief job with the radio orchestra, the film cuts to a long shot of Paul back in his room picking up his violin to practice. For long shots like this, the film shows us the sole, integrated body of actor John Garfield. When the camera cuts to a close-up, however, what we see is a monster whose face and limbs belong to three different beings. We may interpret the intensity with which Paul attacks his instrument as signifying anger and determination, but Negulesco realised that the movie audience can read these emotions better in Garfield's face than in Stern's fingers. The bizarre technique used for these scenes required Garfield to convey emotion solely through his face, a task for which he was well suited.[13]

Decades later, Stern gets to star in his own film on the violin. *From Mao to Mozart* (Murray Lerner, 1980) offers a filmic record of Stern's trip to China. Although the film won an Academy Award for best documentary in 1982, it employs a thoroughly conventional approach to the subject matter. Nevertheless, Carl Plantinga mentions the film in his survey of 1980s documentaries, calling it, in fact, 'among the best' films on music and musicians of that decade (2000: 379). Lerner's camera thoroughly exploits the master violinist's expressive face and *Yiddishe* features, yet those Asian musicians with whom he interacts are represented as proficient but dispassionate instrumentalists.

Consequently, although the film purports to portray Stern as an ambassador of music's universal communicative power, instead what we witness is a representation of a prominent Western musician's failure to appreciate the impact of racial and cultural difference on musical performance.

Stern's voice-over narration informs us that his intent was to visit the country rather than to perform – that the trip was 'less a concert tour than a how-do-you-do, using music as a sort of passport'. Still, Stern graciously assumes the role of instructor and performer when called upon to do so. Unfortunately, the avuncular violinist seems unaware of or unconcerned with his Orientalist biases. His attitude toward Chinese musicians and students is kindly but patronising. Commenting on his rehearsal with the Central Philharmonic, he complains that Chinese musicians are 'not accustomed to playing with passion and variety of colour'.

He casually sweeps aside political issues and avoids debates over ideology. In one scene, the orchestra's conductor speaks of Mozart's place in the transformation from feudalism to modern industrial society. Stern responds that he is skeptical that 'the genius of Mozart had anything to do with the social or economic stage of life at that time'. Rather than situate musical composition within a broader social and political sphere, he retreats to the Romantic notion of exceptional individual genius. Stern's denial is disingenuous considering that his trip was made possible due to the cultural revolution's recent decline, when the appreciation of Western music again becomes permissible. Such circumstances should shake his belief in art's autonomy.[14]

In China, Stern might do well to close his eyes and listen because, whereas he possesses a superior knowledge of Western classical music, the Chinese and their culture puzzle him. He obviously expects emotion to register on the Asian face just as it does on his own very expressive features. During a violin workshop at a Peking conservatory, he prompts an obviously frightened and embarrassed young girl to sing in front of a large audience. Stern shows the girl the correct and incorrect way to render the passage not only by playing his violin but also by changing his facial expression in an exaggerated manner. As he plays a lifeless rendition of the musical phrase, the camera cuts to a tight close-up of him staring ahead stone-faced. Although the Chinese audience laughs at his joke, a serious misapprehension of the Chinese people and their culture actually motivates Stern's demonstration. His expressionless mask is a way of showing how the Chinese face appears to him. Stern's bland stare signifies the lack of passion in the girl's playing, a coldness, Stern believes, that typifies Chinese musicians. It is worth noting that, while Stern makes faces,

Figure 4 – A deadpan Isaac Stern

the girl's eyes remain glued to his fingers, as if she knows that the instrument's sound is produced manually and not through facial contortions.

Another scene shows Stern attending a rehearsal that features pieces from the Peking Opera's repertory. The actors' movements are accompanied by a musical ensemble whose instrumentation would appear unfamiliar to the average Westerner. One of these instruments is the Chinese fiddle, or *erhu*, which belongs to the family of bowed instruments called the *huqin*. Instead of tucking the instrument under the chin, the musician holds the *erhu* with the body resting in the lap or on the knee. The performer's impassive face remains fixed on his instrument. What forces in the history of instrumental performance drew the violin to the face, and what prevented similar developments for the Chinese *erhu*? These are questions for ethnomusicologists. For our purposes, we can note that, instead of facilitating close-ups of the face, this technique calls for wider shots that capture the player from the knees up.

My purpose is not to expose Stern as the 'ugly American' but to demonstrate how privileging the face in music documentaries plays a part in repressing the performer's body. At least since the late Romantic period, facial expression has been regarded as a sign of genuine emotion – of the 'passion' Stern finds missing in the Chinese.

THE ARTLESS DOCUMENTARY

In this next section, I want to take a close look at a documentary dedicated to violin performance: Bruno Monsaingeon's *The Art of Violin*. The film employs talking-head commentary by luminaries such as Itzhak Perlman, Ivry Gitlas and Hilary Hahn along with great quantities of archival footage to construct hagiographies of the modern masters of the violin. A few minutes into the film, we are treated to a long montage of the twentieth-century's greatest violinists playing Felix Mendelssohn's *Concerto in E minor*. Despite the varied sources of the footage, the editors have achieved a nearly seamless effect, gathering these virtuosi together in a musical Valhalla constructed through the cinema. Notwithstanding this masterful cutting, the film has garnered little recognition beyond its worth as an educational tool.

Such neglect is not surprising. Films such as *Monterey Pop* and *Dont Look Back* occupy a secure place in the canon of cinema studies. They appear regularly in histories of documentary and in collections of essays on the subject. Critics treat them as film art as well as records of pop music performances. Many music documentaries, however, fail to attract scholarly attention as films. These numerous films and videos, which fill the catalogues of organisations like the Bel Canto Society, strictly hold interest for musicians and music fans. Almost always marketed under the performer's name, they cannot exploit the celebrity of a star director such as Martin Scorsese or a Jonathan Demme.[15] Nor can such films be grouped into a 'movement' or 'school' of documentary like the work produced by Drew-Leacock and their associates. On one hand, textualist critics find it hard to interpret the content of these movies, which do not – at least overtly – draw on the structure of fictional stories and usually lack character development. On the other, these films resist a formalist approach, composed as they often are of a predictable mixture of performances and interviews. Admittedly, these movies explore no new aesthetic territory, nor do they realise large profits. A perceived lack of commercial potential limits theatrical exhibition, and most are broadcast on cable or public television.[16] Although they may thrill musicians or fans of a featured artist, they bore the average movie spectator looking for an engaging story. Most people find a two-hour film titled *The Art of Violin* about as entertaining as *How to Use a Step Ladder*. No doubt, many music documentaries deserve this reputation. However, Monsaingeon is one director whose work merits wider recognition from cinema scholars. We have already encountered his documentary on Glenn Gould in previous chapters. He has also made several television documentaries on pianist Sviatoslav Richter and singer Dietrich Fischer-Dieskau, as well as *The Art of Violin*.

As a documentary, *The Art of Violin* draws heavily on footage culled from segments in fiction films such as *Hollywood Canteen* (1944) and *Carnegie Hall* (1945). These diverse elements are compiled to form an audio-visual document of modern violin performance styles. The situation is complicated because of the ambiguous status of these segments – are they fiction or nonfiction? They originally appeared in a fictional context, yet they show actual musicians playing their instruments. In fact, these segments would not have much value for documentary if they were not themselves historical documents on film. When these segments become part of documentary cinema proper, they forfeit their entertainment value and gain importance as historical *actualities.* The studio vaults contain a wealth of well-lighted and professionally filmed concert footage.

One such resource is *Hollywood Canteen*, a Warner Bros. wartime musical that consists of musical performances set within a slight narrative frame. Directed by Delmer Daves, this piece of light entertainment is hardly designed to convince the spectator of the story's truth; nevertheless, the boundaries between fiction and nonfiction are blurry here. An establishment called the Hollywood Canteen actual existed then and continues to exist today. Through the efforts of Bette Davis and John Garfield, the original Canteen opened on Cahuenga Boulevard in Los Angeles on 3 October 1942. As in the movie, its primary purpose was to cater to servicemen, and movie stars actually waited on tables and prepared food for patrons. Moreover, despite the corny dialogue and clumsily manufactured coincidences, the movie's story loosely corresponds to actual historical events. *Hollywood Canteen* has an all-star cast, but what makes this movie particularly interesting is that these actors depict themselves. Jack Carson plays Jack Carson the actor – that is, Jack Carson not acting but 'being himself'. The paradox, of course, is that in every scene in which he appears, he *is* acting. All the musicians, of course appear as themselves.

With the exception of violinist Joseph Szigetti, the featured musical performers all belong to the field of popular entertainment rather than that of 'serious' music. Following performances by the likes of the Andrew Sisters and the Jimmy Dorsey Band, the mood turns serious as Davis introduces Szigetti, who performs Schubert's *The Bee.* This very segment also appears in Monsaingeon's *The Art of Violin.* Unfortunately, that film does not show nearly enough of the hilarious duet Szigetti plays with the man Davis introduces as the 'American master of the violin', Jack Benny. Looking at the entire segment in its original fictional context allows us to contrast how a player's face can charge a musical phrase with meaning. Although Szigetti's presence serves to inject a bit of high culture into the proceedings, the segment is not really aimed at classical music buffs; even the greatest philistine in the audience can appreciate Szigetti's virtuosity, his extraordinary command of the instrument made only more obvious when contrasted with Benny's studied incompetence. Of course, Benny's performance also takes considerable skill, in his way of ending a fairly played phrase with an ugly scraping sound without betraying a hint of a smile. Benny understands that one can play a wrong note well.

Straight-faced, Davis introduces Benny as a violin virtuoso. When Szigetti reappears to perform a duet with Benny, he feigns confusion over the latter's identity: 'I thought you were a radio comedian'. Benny responds that, while he dabbles in radio, music is his 'racket'. Following Szigetti's brief interlude of 'serious' music, Benny's performance provides comic relief, to assure that this stuffy 'long-haired' segment does not undermine the movie's popular appeal. When Szigetti suggests they play *Capriccioso* by Saint-Saëns, Benny objects that 'people don't hum it' and insists they play the simple *Souvenir* by Franz Drdla instead. As the two men trade musical phrases, Szigetti's rich sound contrasts with Benny's thin tone and poor intonation. At one point, Benny looks out at the audience and asks, 'Honestly, folks, can you tell the difference?' It would appear that the comedian resorts to mockery to hide his ineptitude, yet the final phrases are rendered sincerely, with beautiful two-part harmony and vibrato. Benny was no professional musician, but he could prevent making a fool of himself if he so desired.

In fact, the young Benjamin Kubelski – the future Jack Benny – had displayed a fair degree of musical talent. But, if he had talent, he certainly lacked the discipline to become a concert musician; instead, he sought his fame in vaudeville, thereby disappointing his mother who had imagined her son another Mischa Elman. Eventually, Benny changed from playing the violin to merely holding it for most of his comedy act. Still, his musical performances became as much a part of his public persona as his miserliness. On his television show, Benny played many comical duets with 'serious' violinists such as Stern and Gisele Mackenzie. Many of these performances can be seen on YouTube and Google Video. One shows Benny and a young Stern playing Bach at Carnegie Hall. Although he seems to play in earnest at first, the well-known comedian has no hope of being appreciated as an earnest musician here. His notoriety as a poor musician has prepared the audience to expect mistakes, and Benny does not disappoint. He falters and seems to lose his place, then stares deadpan at the audience, and once again delivers the line, 'honestly, can you tell the difference?' Stern plays on.

SPEAKING IN STRINGS

If Benny is the stone-faced comic fiddler, violinist Nadja Salerno-Sonnenberg represents his opposite number: a dedicated and talented musician whose wild grimaces have provoked much controversy in the staid world of classical music. Salerno-Sonnenberg's facial tics do not belong to the conventional repertoire of expression. Director Paola di Florio's *Speaking in Strings* (1999) presents Salerno-Sonnenberg as a virtuoso who rejects the acceptably demure feminine approach to performing and incurs the censor of critics for her nonconformity. She has her defenders, of course, such as Allison Ames, vice-president of EMI Classics, who complains that many critics object to the violinist's style because she is 'not poker faced like Heifetz'. The most vociferously disapproving voice to appear in the film is that of Pulitzer prize-winning music critic Martin Bernheimer, who disparages Salerno-Sonnenberg's playing as 'over emoted'. Such criticism of her performance style is certainly polite in contrast to the overtly misogynistic pejoratives such as 'hormonal' that the documentary displays in a montage sequence featuring negative newspaper reviews. Bernheimer also accuses Salerno-Sonnenberg of 'battling the composer rather than interpreting the composer'. By now, this kind of critical discourse should have a familiar ring for us, but it takes on an especially disturbing resonance when uttered by a male critic about a female artist playing the works of male composers (at least all the pieces showcased in di Floria's film were written by men). Such rhetoric evokes ideological notions of man as mind or spirit and woman as body or nature. The ideology cuts both ways. For instance, public relations person Mary Lou Falcone confesses that many people have petitioned her to advise her client to restrain animated bodily movements and facial grimaces. Falcone has consistently declined on the grounds that 'this [Salerno-Sonnenberg's behaviour] was coming from within. This was not external at all. If you start tampering with what is organic in a person, you're tampering with essence.' These comments appeal both to a metaphysical dualism and to an essentialism that casts women as creatures unable to contain their emotions.

One scene shows the violinist performing Prokofiev's 'March' from *Love for 3 Oranges*. She announces the title and begins to lift her instrument to her chin; suddenly, she pauses to add that the piece also served as the theme for television series *The FBI*. Her comedic expression as she delivers this information draws laughter from the audience. When the familiar staccato musical phrase begins, the audience again laughs in recognition. It is important to note that this reaction proceeds from her demeanor and not from the amusing associations that have accrued to the piece itself. Contrast Heifetz playing the same piece in *Heifetz in Performance* (Kirk Browning). As the violinist proceeds, the reserved audience sits watches and listens without a titter.

THE AFFECTION IMAGE AND DIFFERENCE

So far, we have examined the face's role in musical performance in film through historical narratives that employ pairs of oppositions to distinguish acting styles: histrionic code vs. verisimilar code; Saxon vs. Latin styles; Meyerhold's biomechanics vs. Stanislavsky's system; theatrical vs. naturalistic approaches. In addition to these diachronic methods, I propose we add the tool of synchronic analysis taken from philosophy. Unlike the historian, the philosopher works primarily through phenomenological thought processes rather than through archival research, and such methods are not without problems. We will have to evaluate whether the loss of specificity inevitable in such a universalising theory is acceptable.

In *Cinema 1: The Movement-Image*, Gilles Deleuze identifies the close-up of the face with what he calls the *affection image*. Deleuze mixes Belázs's theories on physiognomy with Henri Bergson's philosophy and C. S. Peirce's semiotics. As a result of human evolution, 'the moving body has lost its movement of extension, and movement has become movement of expression ... the Face itself' (1986: 87). This could easily describe the development of acting styles over the last century or so. Following Bergson, Deleuze considers the face a 'plate of nerves', the cinematic close-up revealing 'tiny local movements which the rest of the body usually keeps hidden' (1986: 87; 88). According to the formulation in *Cinema 1*, the face presents itself in two ways: as a unifying contour or as a collection of individual tiny features that resist conglomeration. Another way to put this is to label the face either reflexive or intensive, expressing in turn either a pure quality or a power. We can ask each of these faces an appropriate question: of the reflexive face we inquire, 'what are you thinking about?' Of the intensive face, we ask, 'what is the matter, what do you feel?' (1986: 88). Through minimal movement the reflexive face expresses admiration or wonder; the mobile intensive face expresses desire.

Adopting such a theory would allow us to interpret Isaac Stern's remarkable transformation from manic to deadpan as a change from intensive to reflexive face. It would appear that Jack Benny's face is reflexive through and through, but a closer look at his expression during the duet with Szigetti reveals an intensive series that moves from (feigned) condescension to boredom to smug over-confidence. However, Deleuze also gives us an entirely different way to examine Salerno-Sonnenberg's performances. Her spastic faces represent intensive series of pure power in that they effect qualitative leaps of emotion. We witness her in Abbey Road Studios as she prepares to record the soundtrack to Negulesco's *Humoresque*. Speaking quietly to the camera, she abruptly breaks down and bursts into tears, burying her face in her hands. In a moment, she has gathered enough composure to calmly explain her concern about the recording session. She appears no less volatile in her public performances. Rehearsing and performing Sibelius's *Violin Concerto*, Salerno-Sonnenberg frowns, raises her eyebrows, grins, bares her teeth savagely, then raises her eyes in ecstatic release. When she performs, each musical phrase is accompanied by a set of expressions heading toward a paroxysm of feeling.

The problem is that Deleuze confines his analysis to European and American filmmakers taking as their subject the Western visage (the close-ups of Griffith or Eisenstein, or Dreyer's *tour de force* cinematic treatment of Falconetti's face in *Joan of Arc*). I have been discussing Jewish and Italian faces – the faces of Moses, Christ or the Madonna. We might wonder, however, how well such theories pertain to a non-Western musician such as Midori. The quick response would cast Salerno-Sonnenberg's as the intensive face and Midori's as the reflexive. In fact, however, the latter oscillates between the oval contour of the impassive mask and the knitted eyebrows and pouting lips as an intensive series playing across the pale surface. Deleuze's reference to Griffith's *Broken Blossoms* and Richard Barthelmas's depiction of the Chinese, whose face shows the 'stupor of opium and the reflection of Buddha' (1986: 90). As it was for Stern, the Asian face presents an obstacle to interpretation. Too dangerous to ignore the extent to which cultural difference obscures meaning.

NOTES

1   Maurice Merleau-Ponty calls music 'too far beyond the world and the designatable to depict anything but certain outlines of being' (2003: 293).

2 The present chapter began as an essay on faciality in singing. Singers naturally draw their share of close-ups, and these shots are not always flattering. As Simon Frith notes, 'singing is not necessarily or even desirably pretty – singers sweat, they strain, they open their mouths wide and clench their throats' (1996: 214).

3 In his book on the electric guitar, Steve Waksman refers to Hendrix's Stratocaster as a 'technophallus', a term that signifies 'an electronic appendage that allowed Hendrix to display his instrumental, and, more symbolically, his sexual prowess' (1999: 188).

4 Here, my thought has been influenced by the work of Georges Bataille on human-kind's evolution towards the vertically erect posture and the sacrifices and gains this change entails: 'All the potential for blossoming, all the possibilities for the liberation of energy, now under normal conditions found the way open only toward the superior regions of the buccal orifices, toward the throat, the brain, the eyes. The blossoming of the human face, gifted with the voice, with diverse modes of expression, and with the gaze, is like a conflagration, having the possibility of unleashing immense qualities of energy in the form of bursts of laughter, tears, or sobs; it succeeded the explosiveness that up to that point had made the anal orifice bud and flame' (1985: 77).

5 Cf. also Dziga Vertov (1985), 'We: Variant of a Manifesto'.

6 The phrase comes from Bataille. See note 4 above.

7 Jane Davidson reports on a study of listeners' sensitivity to a singer's use of exaggerated body gestures and 'subtle movements of the eyes and mouth [...] to embody his innermost thoughts and feelings' (2002: 148).

8 See James Naremore on the close-up's role in the ascendance of the natural-ist style and romantic ideology in the Stanislavski System (1988: 40). Naremore quotes Pudovkin emphasising the indispensability of 'extreme paucity of gesture' for Stanislavski (ibid.)

9 See Tom Conley's entry on faciality in *The Deleuze Dictionary* (2005: 96–8).

10 It was D. A. Pennebaker and fellow documentarian Richard Leacock who more-or-less invented light-weight sync-sound equipment by stripping five Auricon cameras and rebuilding them for sync-sound capability with a portable tape deck. The success of the system depended on a camera small enough and light enough to rest on the shoulder instead of on a tripod.

11 There is a link between Jews and the violin, of course. As Sander Gilman notes, 'violin virtuosity has become almost synonymous with Jewish musical genius' (1996: 222). A connection also exists between Jews and Method acting. Although tangential to the present essay, a case could be made to show how musical per-formance and dramatic performance are related through ethnicity .

12 The latter appeals to the gestural systems of Francois Delsarte and Emile Jacques-Dalcroze. For an excellent introduction to Delsarte's and Dalcroze's influence on screen acting see Yampolsky (1996).

13 He had previously demonstrated his skill in under-acting. Consider a scene in *I was a Fugitive* (Mervyn LeRoy, 1933) in which Garfield plays an escaped convict who visits his old cellmate, who gladly gives his pal a room along with some female company. The film cuts between Garfield's expressionless face and the body of the prostitute.

14 In fact, as a bonus feature, the DVD contains the short film *The Gentleman from Shanghai* (Heather Greer), which relates the tribulations of musician Tan Shuzhen, who was demoted from teaching violin to cleaning the conservatory's toilets.

15 This is true even for Maysles films like the films featuring Vladimir Horowitz.

16 See Carl Plantinga's excellent analysis of the economic aspects of American documentary in the 1980s (2000).

INDEPENDENT CINEMA MEETS
FREE JAZZ: SHIRLEY CLARKE'S
ORNETTE: MADE IN AMERICA

Normally, the concert film focuses on a unique event, which might be a single concert, a music festival or an entire tour, the documentation of which provides what Aristotle might call the project's final cause. In contrast, Shirley Clarke's *Ornette: Made in America* (1985) attempts to render neither the circumstances surrounding a particular concert/tour nor present a broad profile of an artist's career. Although the performance of Ornette Coleman's *Skies of America* and the opening of The Performing Arts Center in Fort Worth function as the ostensible motive for the film, its scope exceeds such narrow limits. Refusing to establish the illusion of presence that provides the condition for 'live' performance, Clarke offers up images of change that span generations and geographical locations. Whereas her early dance films had explored the kinematics of the human body in performance, in the *Ornette* film, she explores a broader notion of *kinesis* as change or growth rather than as locomotion only.

The views of emerging science in the Enlightenment obscured the rich meanings formerly attached to *kinesis*, the Greek word from which we derive *cinema*. Aristotle's *Categories*, for instance, lists six kinds of kinesis: generation, decay, increase, diminution, alteration and change of place. It was only in the modern era, when science claimed to explain the body's operations solely in mechanical terms, that kinesis was reduced to locomotion, i.e. change of place, alone (see Aristotle 1936).[1]

Although Shirley Clarke's career spanned more than three decades, her place in the pantheon of independent filmmakers rests on a few critically acclaimed works made in the 1960s. A formally trained dancer, she chose dance as the subject for her first short films in the early 1950s. By the end of the decade, she had won acclaim for a pair of experimental films on New York City architecture: *Bridges Go Round* (1958) and *Skyscraper* (1959). Her first feature film, *The Connection* (1960), an adaptation of Jack Gelber's play about a group of junkies waiting for their dealer, made her easily the most well-known filmmaker of the New American Cinema group.[2] This success and notoriety owed something to the controversy surrounding the censorship of her film. In any case, she entered the 1960s as an established force in cinema and sustained that success throughout that decade. *The Connection* was followed by her Academy Award-winning documentary *Robert Frost: A Lover's Quarrel with the World* (1963), *The Cool World* (1963) and *Portrait of Jason* (1967). Despite such achievements, eighteen years would pass between *Portrait of Jason* and her next feature film, *Ornette: Made in America*.[3] If not precisely a comeback for Clarke – as I shall argue, she had never ceased to thrive as an artist – the film represents a return. That is, it marks her return to film after more than a decade of devoting her energy to education and working in the medium of videotape. It also entailed reviving a project begun in 1968 that she had been forced to abandon: an experimental documentary on legendary jazz musician Ornette Coleman.

A controversial musical figure since his arrival on the scene in the late 1950s, Coleman pioneered the style known as 'free jazz', which liberated improvisation from the traditional harmonic structures that had characterised the post-war jazz style known as bebop. Despite the transformative impact of musicians such as Charlie Parker, Thelonious Monk, Dizzy Gillespie and others, players had remained bound to follow – albeit loosely – the chord changes of Tin Pan Alley's popular tunes. Coleman rejected conventional harmonic structural limits almost entirely while retaining bebop's distinctive rhythmic phrasing. Music critics and fellow musicians responded passionately both for and against his innovations. During his early days in Los Angeles, musicians sometimes walked off the bandstand when Coleman tried to sit in. Others, such as John Lewis of the Modern Jazz Quartet, lent their support and helped Coleman procure recording sessions and live club dates in New York City; gradually, Coleman became accepted.[4]

Like Coleman, Clarke proved a difficult figure for critics to pigeonhole, especially as her career traversed the fields of dance, film, video, theatre and pedagogy. Although she had worked with documentarians D. A. Pennebaker and W. S. Van Dyke, her willingness to employ re-enactments and dramatisations did not jive with the then-reigning ideology of American *cinéma vérité*, which championed unscripted, uncontrolled situations and dictated minimum interference by the filmmaker. Rather than strive for fidelity to unaltered 'reality', Clarke did not shy from mixing documentary and dramatic footage if doing so resulted in a more powerful and believable film. She refused to respect the borders between fiction and nonfiction film and averred that she had 'never made a documentary' because, according to her, no such thing exists (quoted in Rice 1972: 21). Unlike those pursuing greater realism, Clarke preferred to create work that was 'both realistic and abstract at the same time' (quoted in Ward 1982: 23). From its inception, her project on Coleman promised to transcend the genre of the concert film or tour documentary that the public had come to expect from Pennebaker and his direct cinema colleagues.

Certainly, *Ornette: Made in America* takes an unconventional approach to the representation of events and bodies in time. Clarke has sampled moments in Coleman's career and in the maturation of his son, Denardo, who began playing drums in his father's band as a youngster and eventually became Ornette's manager as well. We might say that the film functions as a musical moving picture album of father and son. It also provides a record of its own emergence as a finished film. To a great degree, the meaning of Clarke's film lies not only in its ostensible subject matter but also in the tortured history of its own coming to be – its own actualisation. *Ornette: Made in America* is both a record of Shirley Clarke's aesthetic growth in the post-1960s period as well as a documentary on Ornette and Denardo Coleman. Like other projects actualised over considerable stretches of time (for example, *Metallica: Some Kind of Monster*; Jem Cohen's *Fugazi: Instrument* (1999)), there is a tension between holistic changes to bodies (for instance, addiction and rehabilitation in the Metallica film, or aging in Clarke's) and local bodily movements involved in making music on a instrument.

ORNETTE AND DENARDO

Although *Ornette: Made in America* was released in 1985, work on the project began in 1968. On April 4 of that year, Clarke sent a proposal to David Oppenheim at the Public Broadcasting Laboratory, calling for a three-week shooting schedule and estimating a budget of $50,000 to $60,000. This proposal provides evidence of how much this early effort anticipates the later film. Clarke tells Oppenheim that her film 'will show how music comes into being'; in other words, through moving images she will reveal the mechanism of musical creation as it occurs in improvisation and composition. Clarke also promises to explore the 'new relationship of jazz to classical music', a goal eventually realised when she documents the collaboration between Coleman and the Fort Worth Symphony in 1983. Even as early as 1968, Clarke expresses her intention of looking not only at Ornette but also at his son Denardo, then eleven years old, whom Clarke calls 'a musical genius'. (As a working title, she dubbed the film *Ornette and Denardo.*) Her proposal articulates several questions that revolve around the father/son relationship. Do Ornette and Denardo 'inspire' and 'trust' each other? Are they listening to each other as musicians and as people? How can the father facilitate his son's maturation? How can the son prompt his father to grow and change? Along with these generational changes, another transformation is evident, for, after years of working in the film medium, Clarke was anxious to experiment with the emerging technology of videotape. When Ampex introduced videotape in the 1950s, the equipment was bulky and costly. With the arrival of the Sony Portapak in 1965, however, artists gained access to a portable and relatively affordable machine. As the next decade arrived, Clarke began looking to videotape as her preferred medium.

She constructed a myth to explain her conversion to videotape as primary medium. Although her PBL proposal proves she was already thinking of experimenting with video, her version of events reads like the story of St. Paul on the road to Damascus. According to an interview in the *Los Angeles Weekly Reader*, Clarke reports walking down the street in despair over PBL's decision to abort the Ornette film when she bumped into the owner of the sound studio where she had mixed *The Cool World*. After examining the contents of the box he was carrying, which contained a video camera, Clarke was inspired, and she soon managed to obtain two cameras with a grant from New York State Council on the Arts (see Bebb 1982: 2).

Clarke embraced video and, at least temporarily, discarded the celluloid medium in which she had made her reputation. In 1972, she tells an interviewer categorically that she has abandoned film, that she no longer finds it 'a satisfactory medium', and that 'it doesn't bear a significant relationship to my eye and ear' (quoted in Rice 1972: 21). Video offered her the immediacy film lacked. She recalls the revelation on first setting up her video equipment and training the camera on a friend: 'I did not look through the camera … I looked into the monitor'; the video process allowed her 'to see the finished thing while I was doing it' (quoted in Bebb 1982: 7). This type of real-time interaction suited Clarke, who saw herself as a poor conceptual planner but an adept improviser whose creative powers flourished from hands-on encounters with the materials of her art. Thus, she regarded her video work as the equivalent of a jazz player's improvisations.

Initially, the PBL committed to the Ornette project reservedly, agreeing only to pay Clarke's expenses in order for filming to begin. Negotiations continued, however, and on June 6 Clarke was contracted to deliver a 16mm colour film for television. Still struggling for additional funds, she attempted to pre-sell the British television rights. In a letter to BBC producer Humphrey Burton, she describes the film as exploring the relationship between father and son as well as between 'new techniques in film and TV electronics on the visualisation of sound (how to successfully film music)'. Clarke outlines the film's ambitious itinerary for Burton: it will begin in New York and then move to Coleman's home town of Fort Worth before filming Coleman in concert in San Francisco. Finally, she claims that Coleman will compose music on the computer and the latter will produce complementary visuals. She also relates her plan to include a film-play by Ornette as well as a five-minute film by young Denardo! Whether or not such plans were practical remains a mystery; unfortunately, Burton declined Clarke's request for $15,000 in exchange for rights. A similar scheme to pre-sell the German television rights failed as well, as did her plea for federal government assistance. She was informed not to expect aid from the US State Department's Cultural Exchange Program. Citing budget cuts and a prevailing conservative attitude, Walter Pozen (1968) laments that, at this point in time, 'Louis Armstrong, yes – Ornet [sic] Coleman, no'.

Despite the high regard for the accomplishments of elder musicians like Louis Armstrong, by the late 1960s, the younger generation of players had aligned itself politically with the Black Power movement as well as with the aesthetics of free jazz. For groups such as the Association for the Advancement of Creative Musicians, politics and music were inseparable. Bands such as the Art Ensemble of Chicago embraced African scales and instrumentation and adopted a distinctly African look, wearing African masks, dashikis and skull caps. Many black musicians dropped their 'slave' names in favour of Muslim names. Racial politics, along with protest of the Southeast Asian conflict, emerge as themes in many musical documentaries of the period.

Whether or not a timid reluctance to challenge conservative power affected Public Broadcasting Laboratory's attitude toward Clarke's film, their enthusiasm for the project began to wane. Worrying that 'we may have agreed on an un filmable [sic] subject' (Oppenheim 1968), Oppenheim requested more shooting, stipulating that such additional work cost no more than $5,000. He also delivered an ominous ultimatum: if the new shooting fails to solve the problem, it would be in everyone's interest to cut losses and shelve the film. Finally, PBL pulled the plug, referring to 'the disappointing footage so far'.[5] Luckily, this footage reverted to Clarke, and much of it found its way into *Ornette: Made in America* fourteen years later.

MADE IN/SKIES OF AMERICA

In 1983, the Ornette project was resurrected when Kathelin 'Honey' Hoffman engaged Clarke to film Coleman's performance at the inauguration of the Caravan of Dreams Performing Arts Center in Fort Worth, Texas. Hoffman would be artistic director of the complex, which included a nightclub and a geodesic dome with a cactus garden. The club became an essential venue in downtown Fort Worth for diverse styles of music until it closed in 2001, but the space was originally envisioned as a showcase for blues and jazz, favouring the avant-garde in particular. The opening week's schedule reflected this commitment, beginning with a concert of Coleman's *Skies of America* on 29 September (actually performed at the Tarrant County Convention Centre), followed by Coleman's band Prime Time on 30 September and 1 October, and the world premiere of *Prime Design/Time Design*, the composition for string quartet and percussion that Coleman dedicated to Buckminster Fuller, which was performed in the geodesic dome. The innovative programming continued with jazz drummer Jack DeJohnette on 6–8 October, a retrospective of Shirley Clarke's films on 7 October, and a reading by William Burroughs on 8 October.

As important a role as this inaugural event and its setting play in the film, Clarke insisted that the film is 'about Ornette specifically, not Caravan of Dreams'.[6] True, Coleman's return to his hometown for the *Skies of America* concert and the opening of Caravan of Dreams provided the occasion for Clarke's film. Nevertheless, the film refuses to remain in 1983 and in Fort Worth, continually pushing the limits of the here and now. Shots of Coleman's Prime Time band and the Fort Worth Symphony alternate with scenes from Clarke's unfinished film from the 1960s, as well as with archival footage from the 1970s and 1980s featuring Coleman performing in places as diverse as Milan, Nigeria and Morocco. Because so many scenes present Coleman as world artist rather than US citizen, the film's title, *Made in America*, seems especially ironic. In fact, Clarke cuts between various performances so often that even the most observant spectator would have difficulty telling where and when the film takes place.

The performance of Ornette's *Skies of America* in his hometown of Fort Worth does impart a certain aura of uniqueness or exclusiveness to the occasion. However, while the performance occurred in 1983, the musical piece, composed for symphony orchestra and jazz ensemble, had been written over a decade before, in 1971, and Coleman had in fact recorded it with the London Philharmonic Orchestra for CBS records the following year. Unfortunately, problems with the British Musicians Union had prevented his band from participating in that session, and Coleman had been forced to revise the score extensively. Thankfully, the jazz quartet and expurgated sections were restored for the composition's public premiere at the Newport in New York Jazz Festival, July 1972. Thus, Clarke's film provides a record of *Skies of America*, but not a definitive one, for the 1983 version differed considerably from the earlier New York version. In subsequent performances, the piece has continued to evolve.

By the time he wrote *Skies of America*, Coleman had abandoned his free jazz style for a mix of progressive jazz and funk based on an eccentric theory of creativity he called *harmolodics*. Also, by the mid-1970s, he no longer performed with acoustic trios and quartets but had recruited electric instrumentalists for an unusual line-up consisting of dual trios of drums, bass and guitar. By 1978, the band's personnel had more or less settled, with Bern Nix and Charles Ellerbe on guitars, Jamaaladeen Tacuma and Albert MacDowell on basses, and Sabiara Kamal and Denardo Coleman on drums. It is this ensemble that Coleman fronted in the 1983 Fort Worth concert that appears in *Ornette: Made in America*.

We might say that this performance at the Convention Center provides a nucleus around which various segments orbit. The latter are sometimes announced by the crawling text that Clarke uses to identify historical periods, events, places and people. Segments marked in this way are: NEW YORK 1968; FATHER AND SON 1984; A MUSICAL JOURNEY BEGINS; MARTIN LUTHER KING'S MARCH ON WASHINGTON 1968; 'ARTIST'S HOUSE' NYC 1972; THE MUSICIANS OF NIGERIA; 'THE LINK' SATELLITE CONNECTION BETWEEN LOWER MANHATTAN AND HARLEM. Many of these scenes function as 'flashbacks', though not all refer to prior events. For instance, although the show opening the Caravan of Dreams nightclub is marked by the change

Figure 5 – Guitarist Bern Nix at the Convention Center in Fort Worth...

of setting, it flashes forward rather than backward in time, since the event occurred the night after the *Skies of America* concert. Clarke frustrates linear chronology further by cutting between visual images taken from both these performances while maintaining the soundtrack's continuity. A particularly dazzling example of this effect occurs on a graphically matched cut on the figure of guitarist Bern Nix. In the first shot, taken during one of the night-club performances on 30 September or 1 October, the camera captures Nix from over his left shoulder as he bends over his instrument. A swish pan to the left resolves in another shot from a nearly identical angle and distance but now showing Nix on stage at the Convention Center the previous night (29 September). Both these visual images occur in sync with a seamless audio track. Here, Clarke employs a technique adopted from her earliest film, *Dance in the Sun* (1953), in which she cuts dancer Daniel Nagrin in the middle of a gesture between two locations, the studio and the beach. The juxtaposition has the effect of a jump cut, but its meaning goes beyond mere formal play-fulness. By showing Nix's body executing nearly identical movements in two different places on two consecutive nights, Clarke is demonstrating that even radical improvisers work within familiar territory. Repetition guarantees that a musical work retains its identity through various performances (although identity does not necessarily depend on fidelity to an authoritative written score, as Nelson Goodman has suggested (1976: 179–92]).[7]

Figure 6 – ... and at the Caravan of Dreams

The movie begins with the mayor of Fort Worth giving Ornette the key to the city. This scene gives way to members of Prime Time discussing this ceremony backstage, and from there we proceed to the Symphony Hall stage. Any expectation that we will be watching a conventional concert documentary quickly vanishes, however, as the film cuts to various dramatic reenactments featuring two young actors, Demon Marshall and Eugene Tatum, whom Clarke employed to play Ornette as a child and as a teenager. These actors sometimes enact entire scenarios, the historical veracity of which is questionable. In the first such scene, a caption fulfills the referential function: THE HOUSE ORNETTE WAS BORN IN. Without the crawling titles that accompany certain images, nothing would identify them as depicting actual incidents and people from Coleman's past.

Just as images of the true Ornette are mixed with those of the boys portraying him as a youth, images of Denardo merge with his father's past and present. At one point, we see Ornette and son in New York, 1968, discussing Denardo's future as an artist and his improvisational method. This shot gives way to a rehearsal session filmed around the same period featuring Ornette, Denardo and bassist Charlie Haden. Next, we get an overhead shot of the young 'Ornette' walking by a railroad crossing in Fort Worth – a scene filmed in the present but representing the past. Cut to a shot of the adult Denardo walking towards the tracks. Denardo turns and looks towards the camera, arousing our expectations for a point-of-view shot. Instead, the camera position and angle remain fixed and render the exact same shot of his father, as if the one person had been transformed into the other – a stop-motion trick as old as the films of Georges Méliès. The following shot shows father and son talking on the porch of Ornette's childhood home. As Ornette relates an anecdote from his childhood, the film shows the young 'Ornette' walking by the tracks. After another shot of the train, the film returns to the Fort Worth concert and Denardo playing a train-like rhythm on the high hat.

FATHER AND SON; MOTHER AND DAUGHTER

These two musicians, father and son, are linked through the most ancient, carbon-based technology: genetic inheritance. Indeed, shared bloodlines is a pervasive theme throughout the film. The communication between generations is literalised in the segment entitled 'The Link'. Although it appears in Shirley Clarke's film, 'The Link' clearly belongs to her daughter Wendy, who conceived the piece and designed the installation, which involved setting up a satellite hookup between New York's World Trade Center and the Adam Clayton Powell Center in Harlem for the month of June 1984. Several events were featured at the two sites, including a duet by Ornette and Denardo, with the former downtown and the latter uptown. Thus, the installation explicitly challenged the limits of physical space. In the segment that appears in *Ornette: Made in America*, one spectator's comment reflects the performance's challenge to traditional notions of presence: 'I think it's great that musicians can get together without being together'. 'The Link' celebrates technology's potential for facilitating telecommunication between interlocutors, anticipating the long-distance jam sessions available through the Internet in recent years. The segment's inclusion here illustrates Shirley Clarke's interest in dialogue and interactive media, 'all to get ready for the world-wide communications web'.[8] This prediction proved prescient, and we might speculate about what she might have produced if she had lived to explore the Internet's possibilities.

It is hard not to see the parallels between Shirley/Wendy's relationship and Ornette/Denardo's. This film addresses the connection between generations in several ways: father and son, mother and daughter, teacher and student. (Clarke even takes care to include a conversation between Denardo and his mother, poet Jayne Cortez, later in the film.) Both Ornette Coleman and Shirley Clarke bequeath impressive legacies to their offspring: Denardo finds his place in Ornette's bands while Wendy becomes a member of her mother's

Tee Pee Videospace Troupe (more on this below). Both parents praise their children rather shamelessly, if honestly. One scene shows Ornette conversing with his grown son on the porch of the Fort Worth house that was Ornette's birthplace. Here, Ornette elaborates on what he considers valuable in music: he is inspired by a player who can create music that differs from what everybody else is doing. He adds the remarkable claim that Denardo does this better than anybody else – even better than himself. Likewise, in a written interview between mother and daughter, Shirley tells Wendy that she is 'representative of the young artists who are finding the perfect media for their multi-talents and multi-skills.' Better still, the film provides a sample of Wendy Clarke's work in 'The Link' segment.[9]

Just as Denardo surpasses his father's efforts to improvise freely, one could argue that 'The Link' more accurately represents what Shirley Clarke was attempting to do in the 1970s than any other segment in *Ornette: Made in America*. In the decade or so preceding that film, Clarke had devoted her energy to experimental, multi-channel video performances, beginning with a series of live, multi-channel video events – we might think of them as 'happenings' – at her rooftop apartment in New York's Chelsea Hotel. These gatherings constituted a modern-day 'salon', with visiting celebrities such as Arthur C. Clarke, Gene Youngblood and Ornette himself. From these events a core group emerged, which included Wendy Clarke, Andy Gurian and Bruce Ferguson as the most regular participants. Clarke dubbed this collective the Tee Pee Videospace Troupe after the rooftop structure where the members had met (see Gurian 2004). Not confined to the roof of the Chelsea Hotel, the Tee Pee Videospace Troupe – Clarke's 'band' we might consider it – took their video workshops/performances on the road. Unfortunately, the troupe fell apart when Clarke left New York to teach at UCLA. Once in California, she adopted a healthy lifestyle; in an interview taped for a student cable show, we see her eating carrot sticks and calling herself 'reformed.' In the early 1980s, just before the *Ornette: Made in America* film, she returned to New York Women's Interart Center to work with actor Joseph Chaiken and author Sam Shepard, a collaboration that resulted in a pair of videotapes: *Tongues* (1982) and *Savage Love* (1981). These tapes feature dramatic monologues delivered by Chaiken.

Innovative in their own right,[10] these single-channel videos nevertheless differ significantly from her previous work with Tee Pee. In fact, Andy Gurian has expressed his surprise and disappointment regarding Clarke's return to single-channel video work.[11] Indeed, her move seems regressive considering her categorical proclamations about video's radical potential as a new medium. She laments that 'some will use video to make films,' and then adds that 'some, I hope, will use video to make video.' The rhetoric of those statements, however, should be read along with Clarke's later plans: a never-realised film adaptation of Lewis John Carlino's play *Snowangel* that would star Shelley Winters, talk of adapting Joan Didion's *Book of Common Prayer*. These ideas suggest that Clarke had begun to revise her earlier position that film no longer interested her. Nevertheless, these in no way negate her dedication and contribution to video. Parry Teasdale, one of the founders of Videofreex collective, calls Clarke the strongest influence on his perception of the medium. According to Teasdale, 'Millions of people knew video as television, and television only as its passive receptors. ... Shirley, more than all the video groups and all the studiously academic video artists, possessed a truly revolutionary vision for turning television on its head' (1999: 116; 120).

SHIRLEY CLARKE, VIDEOGRAPHER

Ornette: Made in America in fact contains its share of videotaped segments: for instance, Prime Time's appearance at the dance club in Fort Worth and the performance of Ornette's chamber piece, *Prime Time/Time Design*, which was shot in the geodesic dome (referred to as the 'Cactus Video' because of the variety of desert plants on display there). Significantly, audio record-ings of these performances were released on the Caravan of Dreams label.[12] Apparently, the symphony demanded film – the 'legitimate' medium – while the small ensemble pieces allowed for experimentation with videotape. Clarke also obtained video footage from NASA over which she superimposes images of Ornette traveling through space in various vehicles. The brief segment 'Ornette Coleman – A Jazz Video Game' explores a variety of video effects including feedback, chroma keying and debeaming.[13] The segment begins with actor Demon Marshall in a video arcade playing TRON. The electronic noise of the game mixes with Ornette's solo saxophone, just as the game's screen appears under various images. A brief scenario unfolds, featuring the young 'Ornette' drawn into a cave by a dazzling star, playing with marbles in dirt, and standing behind the neon circle, square and triangle that forms the Caravan of Dreams logo. Video feedback techniques show us multiple images of Ornette playing his horn before returning to the video arcade where Eugene Tatum is demonstrating his skill in the dance that used to be called 'poppin''. The segment ends with multiple images of Ornette smiling, which give way to a final text signaling, 'game over'. The entire 'interlude' seems designed to showcase the potential of video effects.

While I have referred to the film as a sort of home-movie, it would be wrong to think of *Ornette: Made in America* as conforming to a DIY aesthetic in the same way as, say, Jem Cohen's extensive portrait of the band Fugazi. A glance at the production schedule for the two-hour shoot of the concert at the Convention Center reveals that Clarke had an arsenal of equipment along with the experienced crew to operate it, including four Aaton super-16mm cameras with four cameramen, four camera assistants, two film loaders, two sound men each with a stereo Nagra tape deck, a gaffer, key grip, production manager, and so forth.

After more than fifteen years dedicated to exploring the medium of video-tape, the return to film was not easy for Clarke. In a videotaped interview that takes place in the geodesic dome, she admits to feeling 'scared' about using film and confesses that doing so was not her decision. To a significant degree, she purchased insurance by hiring Ed Lachman as director of photography. Lachman already possessed a considerable reputation from his work with Werner Herzog, Wim Wenders and others. The movie's credits read like a who's who of legendary cinematographers, with supplementary camerawork by Baird Bryant (most famous, perhaps, for capturing the killing of Meredith Hunter in the Maysles brothers' *Gimme Shelter*) and Hillary Harris. Nevertheless, a project such as this, developed over such a considerable period and utilising such diverse source material, was bound to present difficulties in compatibility among the various capture media. For instance, the recent footage consisting of Convention Center and Dome performances, shot in Super 16mm, had to be integrated with older segments of 16mm reversal film. In addition, there were several videotape formats, with and without time code. The soundtrack also presented problems. No separate audio tapes existed for the video work, so the entire soundtrack had to be converted to a 16mm magnetic master, which then had to be resynchronised with the visuals. Of course, switching formats while minimising loss of fidelity presented a challenge. Clarke had completed a ¾' video cut of the film, but this could only serve as a guide because of the low resolution of this format.

Like most music documentaries, *Ornette: Made in America* resorts to talking-head interviews, a cliché that Clarke undermines by placing each speaker in the screen of a crudely drawn television set. These interviews juxtapose official history with legend. Composer George Russell's portrait of Coleman as iconoclast works against *New York Times* critic John Rockwell's attempt to situate Coleman within the 'tradition' of musical modernism, in other words, within the musical history of the West.[14] Rockwell compares Coleman's music with 'any kind of music' that challenges mainstream tastes, sandwiching free jazz between 'modernist classical music' and 'punk rock'. By linking public resistance to such musical styles with their formal innovations, Rockwell elides the issues of race and class so central to these diverse cultural and social movements. In contrast, Russell wants to know how the musicians in Coleman's band can begin to play at the same time despite the absence of someone counting off. Coleman replies simply, 'insight', an inter-subjective perception that Russell muses might be an instance of 'third-world technology'. Note the differences between Rockwell and Russell here: whereas the former tries to establish diachronic succession – who follows whom in music history – Russell foregrounds synchronicity, articulating the concerns of improvisers working outside Western practices: how do we begin at the same moment? These are the types of questions about improvisational methods Ornette puts to his young son in the 1968 New York interview cited above. 'You're more right than you are wrong', he assures his son, but from what criteria do right and wrong judgements derive? The question as to how one can make a mistake in a situation of nearly unlimited freedom often troubled Ornette, even as it legitimised his theory.

Ornette believes his son possesses greater insight than himself because Denardo's freedom has been nurtured. Belonging to the younger generation of jazz percussionists who refuse the traditional role of time-keeper, Denardo plays *with* rather than *under* the other musicians. In classical music, a conductor (such as Giordano) fulfills the function of 'counting off', monitoring the tempo and keeping the musicians 'in concert'. Although a large symphony orchestra necessitates such centralised management, a small jazz ensemble renders the *maestro* obsolete. In Clarke's film of *Skies of America*, this becomes apparent in those sections where the band takes over, the orchestra sits silently and Giordano looks on uncomfortably. In his 'television' interview, Giordano acknowledges how Coleman's philosophy clashes with the symphony orchestra as an institution that requires players to repress the audio and visual signs of their individual styles in order to blend with the ensemble.

The fact that collective improvisation can work with even large ensembles is one difference between the regimented organisation of Western 'serious' music and other cultures. In Clarke's film, much is made of the journey to Nigeria that Rockwell acknowledges as a transformative experience for Coleman. Backstage, we see Ornette discussing with Brion Guysin and

William Burroughs their trip to Morocco in 1973. Musician and critic Robert Palmer describes the large ensemble, which consisted of fifteen horns and fifteen drummers. Luckily, Clarke had located footage of Coleman playing with Hausa musicians during his trip to Nigeria in 1972, and she cut this footage into scenes of Coleman and cornetist Don Cherry performing in New York, with the percussion from the Nigeria film continuing under the sound of the New York performance. During that African trip, Coleman, along with an ensemble of Joujouka musicians, had recorded music in a ritually consecrated cave for an album to be called, appropriately, *Music From the Cave*. Unfortunately, CBS records decided not to release the recording. The promotional one-sheet for the film announces that the soundtrack is available on CBS Records. No doubt, this 'soundtrack' refers to the 1972 recording mentioned above and not to the actual music in the film.

KINEMATICS

Whether done intentionally or not, the focus on Denardo provides the answer to Clarke's question of 'how to film music'. In her early film career, she had explored the problem of filming dance. Perhaps the two problems are not so different if we conceive of musical movement in terms of *performance* rather than those of *composition*. In the late 1960s, Clarke imagined Ornette Coleman making 'visual music' on a computer, possibly resulting in the abstract arabesques typical of animators such as Oskar Fischinger or Len Lye – effects that today have been rendered banal by the digital music 'visualisation' programmes of iTunes and Windows Media Player. Yet the body of the performing musician is the often overlooked, yet obvious, connection between the organised sound we call music and physical movement, and, if the mechanics of saxophone playing remain hidden from the camera's lens, those of the percussionist are clearly visible. This physical connection has been repressed in favour of musical movement conceived in terms of the trajectory of a tone in two-dimensional space. The rise of a sophisticated notational system in the West has perpetuated this notion of the musical score as a representation of abstract moving objects rather than as a set of written instructions for performers (see Shove & Repp 1996; Baily 1985). And yet it is the latter who actually produce the music we hear; it is Denardo's body that strains and sweats as he beats his drums, his hand wrapped with bandages that mark the fleshy interface where performer encounters instrument. Clarke's film keeps this human motion visible on screen and also gives us verbal testimony pertaining to the frailty of the musician's body, for instance, when a concerned Denardo describes the punctured lung his father suffered during a mugging in front of his Lower East Side building. We are reminded that the unique sound we identify with Ornette Coleman begins in those organs deep in his chest, and the graphic details Denardo relates of this beating show how easily violence could silence this sound.

Inevitably, time will wreak its own brutal havoc on Coleman's body, and Clarke's film will remain as one of the few audio-visual records of him performing and speaking. At present, *Ornette: Made in America* is a hard film to find, and I know of no plans to distribute it properly, that is, with treatment comparable to the 2005 DVD release of *Portrait of Jason* by Second Run.[15] Thankfully, the Center for Film and Theater Archive at the University of Wisconsin has video copies available for viewing, and UCLA has proposed an extensive restoration and archival project of Clarke's body of work. Nevertheless, the film's absence from public circulation deprives not only jazz and cinema connoisseurs but also a broader audience of what is possibly the most innovative of music documentaries. Besides documenting an important musical performance, *Ornette: Made in America* represents the meeting of two major figures in the avant-garde of the late twentieth century. It is also Shirley Clarke's final feature-length film, and no assessment of her status as an auteur would be complete without it.

NOTES

1   This definition is somewhat crude but sufficient for present purposes. For a more nuanced discussion of Aristotle's concept of motion and the terms *entelechy* and *energeia*, see Joe Sachs' entry in the *Internet Encyclopedia of Philosophy*.

2   In fact, Clarke was the lone woman signatory of the New American Cinema group's 1961 manifesto, which rejected Hollywood's big-budget, industrial mode of production in favour of an intensely personal cinema. See New American Cinema Group (2000).

3   On Clarke's early career, see Lauren Rabinovitz (2003); see also James Kreul (2004).

4   Derek Bailey quotes saxophonist Steve Lacy on Coleman as iconoclast: 'When Ornette hit the scene, that was the end of the theories. He destroyed the theories. I remember at that time he said, very carefully, "Well, you just have a certain amount of space and you put what you want in it"' (1992: 55). For an overview of Coleman's life and career, as well as a comprehensive discography, see Peter Niklas Wilson's biography (1999).

5   Frederick M. Bohen and Av Westin to Clarke, 16 October 1968. Shirley Clarke

Papers.

6 Clarke, notebook (August 21–2); Shirley Clarke Papers.

7 See section V, 'Score, Sketch, and Script', especially subsection 2, 'Music', of Goodman's *Languages of Art* (1976: 179–92).

8 *L.A. Interchange* interview.

9 On Wendy Clarke's work, see Michael Renov (2004).

10 Deirdre Boyle counts these works among the 'classics' in her *Video Classics: A Guide to Video Art and Documentary Tapes* (1986: 130–2).

11 Andy Gurian to the author. Email exchange. 11 September 2006.

12 Ornette Coleman and Prime Time, *Opening the Caravan of Dreams*, CDP85001; Ornette Coleman, *Prime Time/Time Design*, Denardo Coleman with the Gregory Gelman Ensemble, CDP 85002.

13 Today, when every camcorder offers an array of such effects, it is hard to imagine them as 'special'. For an explanation of these terms and for an idea of the promise they held during video's early years, see the chapter 'Cathode-Ray Tube Videotronics' in Gene Youngblood's *Expanded Cinema* (1970: 265–80).

14 Rockwell's comments fall in line with the proponents of so-called Third Stream music, a cross-over style between jazz and classical, who embraced Coleman's music. Coleman had collaborated previously with the doyen of Third Stream, Gunther Schuller, on records such as *Jazz Abstractions*. Derek Bailey argues that 'free jazz' became rigid and conventional as jazz became an institution seeking to present 'a respectable "official" face authenticated by a phalanx of academics and propagandists, an authority to counter-balance the institutional and academic authority of white classical music' (1992: 56).

15 *Portrait of Jason: A Film by Shirley Clarke*, dir. Shirley Clarke, 99 minutes, Second Run, 2005, DVD. The DVD also contains selections from Wendy Clarke's *Love Tapes*.

'I'M LOOKING AT THEM AND THEY'RE LOOKING AT ME': OBSERVATION AND COMMUNICATION IN *SEX PISTOLS: LIVE AT THE LONGHORN*

In the realm of artistic practice, punk effected a reversal of received aesthetic criteria by investing amateurism with the value normally awarded professionalism. In lieu of arcane rites of passage,[1] a simple recipe sufficed for impatient punk rockers: here's a chord; here's another and another; now form a band. The 'do it yourself' ethos of punk inspired filmmakers as well as musicians. While the official media adopted a hostile attitude toward punk rock, sympathetic chroniclers emerged from the movement's own rank and file. One of these was Don Letts, then disc jockey at the Roxy club in London. Letts relates how he came to filmmaking:

> The Pistols were doing something, instead of the hero worship, I thought, Hey, I can do it too. … I couldn't play anything anyway, so I picked up a super-8 camera, inspired by Johnny Lydon. I didn't know what the hell I was doing, but somebody from the media saw me and wrote, 'Don Letts is making a film.' Hey, that's not a bad idea. Jeanette [Lee] used to help me with the lights, and I'd run the camera. My only talent was I knew what to point it at. (Quoted in Lydon 1994: 272)

Here Letts describes himself making the punk gesture *par excellence*: possessing neither technical proficiency acquired through practice nor certifiable mastery bestowed by formal training, he picks up his chosen instrument (a camera instead of a guitar) and gets on with it.

Given this emphasis on action rather than on reflection, the fact that so many documentaries on punk have come to rely on talking-head interviews strikes me as odd. Such practices are not unusual in documentary, of course. Historiography purports to mold messy events into neat narratives, and verbal testimony accomplishes this job more effectively than music and images. Pursuing a story, however, the filmmaker can lose sight of the value of performances. In general, documentaries on punk aim to chronicle a broad social and artistic movement, international in scope and evolving through time – a goal both worthy and necessary. However, as attention turns to the turf wars of the past three decades, the provisional answers to questions such as *Who started punk? Where did it begin? What were its influences?* have begun to congeal into legend. Particularly polemical are those films trying to penetrate the still smoking ruins of punk's most infamous band: The Sex Pistols. Ex-manager Malcolm McLaren's heavy hand undercuts the documentary value of *The Great Rock 'n' Roll Swindle* (Julien Temple, 1980). In *The Filth and the Fury* (2000), Temple redeems himself somewhat by offering a rejoinder to the *Swindle* film. However, that film's obsequious promotion of John Lydon as Guardian of Truth compromises its credibility. A long introductory segment of newsreel from the 1970s with voice-over narration (mostly) by Lydon effectively establishes his trademark nasal whine as the film's authoritative voice. 'Two sides to every story', Lydon would come to sing in 'Public Image', the initial single from PIL, his post-Pistols project, but it would appear that the one and true story is won through a dialectical struggle, in which Lydon takes the antithetical position opposite McLaren's thesis. *The Filth and the Fury* represents not only the antithesis, however, but the sublation, which purifies the story and leaves the untruths behind.[2]

I realise that, in many ways, the very strategies I have been criticising could be celebrated as representative of documentary cinema at its best: a rhetorical medium that facilitates the staging of debates over social issues. Nevertheless, I cannot help but regard this urge to set the record straight with suspicion and even a little disdain. As I made my way through the continually mounting pile of movies on punk while writing this book, I became convinced that, like the music itself, the best films are raw and messy: Julien Temple and John Tiberi's *Sex Pistols Number 1* (1978; released on video as *Buried Alive*), Lech Kowalski's *D.O.A.* (1980), Ivan Kral and Amos Poe's *Blank Generation* (1976), Penelope Spheeris's *The Decline of Western Civilization* (1981), Jem Cohen's *Fugazi: Instrument* (1999) and *Sex Pistols: Live at the Longhorn* (1995).

Given the heavy burden of legend, it is useful to bracket the commentary – the personal testimony, the interviews, and voice-over narration – and attempt a formal analysis of a film dedicated to a single live performance. In isolation, that film can appear as a singular unity, which can then be analysed to yield further distinctions. *Sex Pistols: Live at the Longhorn* makes a good subject for such a case study: it contains no interviews, backstage conversations, voice-over narration or archival photographs. It possesses another advantage by lacking auteur status. Whereas Temple and Letts have acquired some degree of renown as directors,[3] the Warner Bros. crew responsible for shooting the Dallas show remains anonymous. This fact frustrates attempts to incorporate the film within a director's corpus.[4]

No interviews, voice-over or authorial interventions: have I just described the type of filmmaking called observational? If so, I hope the mere mention of such an approach does not put readers off. The shortcomings of observational cinema have been well broadcasted – its pretensions to scientific objectivity along with a naïve belief that truth will emerge spontaneously through the patient and unobtrusive recording of events. Despite producing an impressive body of compelling and entertaining films, the observational mode perpetrated many abuses, exploiting spectators' voyeuristic curiosity regarding the private moments of other people's lives while disavowing the filmmakers' intervention. But compare Letts's statement above about his 'only talent' to D. A. Pennebaker's confession that 'if there's any artistry in what I do, it is deciding who to turn this fearsome machinery on'; in her essay on *Dont Look Back*, Jeanne Hall offers this quotation to demonstrate how Pennebaker credits Dylan and not himself for 'breaking through' to disclose the truth (see Hall 1998: 227). An equally valid reading of Pennebaker's modest disclaimer, however, equates 'artistry' (or, in Letts's words, 'talent') with the activities of distinguishing and indicating.

Film studies has most often treated *observation* with suspicion or scorn. Critics aver that filmmakers strive for unobtrusive shooting and editing that relates a story without noticeable traces of inscription in order to distract the spectator, who is 'sutured' into the text through unconscious identification with a gaze that is typically gendered masculine. This model holds true not merely for fiction film produced in the classical mode for theatrical exhibition but for ethnographic works employed for pedagogical situations. For example, professor of anthropology Jay Ruby admits defeat in prompting his students to adopt an active, critically engaged attitude toward film due to the 'several-thousand-year-old theatrical/filmic tradition of passive attention' (2008: 6). As we move from exhibition to documentary production, a close look at the critical discourse reveals how observation has accrued associations with passivity. Consider, for example, the work of Brian Winston, certainly a vociferous critic of direct cinema's influence on documentary (1995; 2000). I do not intend to set up such a thorough scholar as Winston as a straw man. Without stereotyping – on the contrary, insisting that the actual practices of direct cinema rarely conformed to the exaggerated discourse – Winston traces direct cinema's part in the development of 'a journalistic ethic of non-intervention and strict observation'; he goes on to note that documentary's creativity 'was becoming increasingly suspect as the requirement for strict observation replaced it' (2000: 22; 23). Notice how these statements link 'non-intervention' with 'strict observation'. Note also Richard Allen and Douglas Gomery's description of the *vérité* filmmaker as 'a neutral observer' (1985: 223). In such formulations the observer occupies a passive and distant stance in regard to events in the pro-filmic world. Even those supporters such as William Rothman perpetuate the *vérité* filmmakers as 'observers who wait selflessly for the people they are filming to reveal themselves' (1996: 8).

I want to suggest that we might rehabilitate the epithet 'observational' by examining how the concept of the observer operates in modern systems theory as developed by Niklas Luhmann, Francisco Varela, Humberto Maturana and others.[5] Observation is the very keystone of *systems theory* discourse. All knowledge results from the actions of an embodied observer, who performs the interdependent processes of distinguishing and indicating. Systems theory avoids making claims concerning essential ontological identities. Based in the 'hard' science of biology, it does seek scientific validation for its theories, but with the caveat that scientific explanations refer to the experience of the observer and not to an independent reality. That is not to deny the existence of a world 'out there'. Indeed, as Maturara insists, 'the natural world is in its spontaneous presence the proof of its own existence'. Access to such a world, however, cannot occur immediately but only becomes available through the experience of an observer or several observers.

In this chapter, I want to examine the rock music concert as the kind of formal organisation that systems theorists have dubbed *autopoietic*. Originally applied to biological organisms, the term has been adapted to describe a variety of social phenomena.[6] Simply put, autopoietic systems are bounded entities that produce those components that allow the system to perpetuate itself. I want to draw attention to the admittedly obvious fact that, to continue to exist, the industry needs to manufacture (among other things) rock stars and their fans. It needs to produce both continuously, to distinguish clearly between them, and to safeguard this distinction. For that distinction's disintegration would jeopardise the organisation that allows the industry to persist as such. I want to emphasise again that such a distinction is relative to an embodied observer and not a timeless, universal fact. For instance, pioneer ethnomusicologist John Blacking (1973) has pointed out the paradox that, according to capitalist dogma, some people are musical while others are not, yet capitalist practice proves otherwise. That is, for the artists' music to be appreciated, their audience must possess a comparable degree of musical proclivity.

We must be wary of considering the audience as a component of the music industry, however, for it actually lies outside the system's boundaries as *environment*. Another way to put it is that a band's so-called fan base constitutes a distinct autonomous unity, which interacts with the industry to form a network in which behaviour in one provokes changes of state in the other. Such interaction is known as *structural coupling*. Unlike the computational model, in which the system receives information to be processed and returned, in an autopoietic model changes in the environment trigger structural changes in the system. If these two congruent unities (system and environment) interact such that the system's organisation persists – in other words, if adaptation occurs – the two have achieved successful structural coupling. If, however, the environment sparks structural changes in the system that disrupt its organisation, the system disintegrates as a unity and loses its identity. In sum, a system's ontogenetic development depends on its adaptability; its organisation must remain intact even as structural components change.

The economic structure of the music industry requires that consumers exchange money for product. The company hopefully makes a profit and reinvests in its roster of artists. We might view the industry, then, as a *heteropoietic* machine (like a jukebox) that effects a transduction so that money goes in and music comes out ('music for money' as Nick Lowe expressed it in the song by that name). In systems theory terms, however, consumer purchasing would be a form of behaviour that triggers changes in the industry. Note that the evolution of structural components may evolve without causing fatal damage – i.e. it is of no consequence whether fans purchase LPs, CDs or MP3s – as long as the system's organisation is allowed to persist. If recording formats are fungible, so are the bands themselves and, to an extent, the individuals who comprise them.[7] But the industry cannot thrive without idols and their worshippers. As purchasers of musical recordings, the audience functions as generators of profit, which company accountants can treat as abstract statistics. In the concert hall, however, the mutual presence of musicians and audience calls for immediate practical steps to distinguish the rock stars from their audience. During the first years of the decade (the 1970s), increasingly, stars performed to adoring fans. Until punk came along.

DESTROY: the word emblazoned across Johnny Rotten's chest supplied punk with its motto. The movement – if it can be described as such – constructed no positive political platform. Punk attitude – I hesitate to call it a philosophy – was essentially reactive and critical. A tactical agenda existed, but there were no definite criteria for victory. ('I don't know what I want but I know how to get it', Rotten sang in 'Anarchy in the UK'.) Nevertheless, battle lines were clearly drawn and the enemy distinctly targeted. One's allegiance could be declared on a T-shirt, like the one Paul Cook is seen wearing in the 'God Save the Queen' promo, which states: 'I Hate Pink Floyd'. Dethroning the rock star and rejecting the excesses of the rock & roll lifestyle allowed these new bands to distinguish themselves from their established elders. Distancing themselves from stardom also promoted solidarity between punk musicians and fans who, like the bands themselves, were generally poor and working class. 'I don't need a Rolls Royce', Rotten announces in Temple and Tiberi's early film on the Pistols, *Number 1*. He insists that he has no need of heroes, and dismisses them all as 'useless'.[8] In our current day of American Idols and Guitar Heroes, such iconoclastic pretensions seem quaint. But Rotten's misunderstanding of the difference between anarchy and nihilism aside, he knew how to marshal the power of the negative.

LIVE AT THE LONGHORN

Despite the remarkable emergence of popular music phenomena during the 1950s and 1960s – SUN records and Elvis, Motown, the Beatles and the British Invasion, the West-coast psychedelic bands, to name just a few – only in the 1970s did rock become established as an institution. In the 1960s small independent companies were absorbed by major labels, which in turn merged into conglomerates like WEA (Warners-Electra-Atlantic). These giants could draw on vast resources in print, television, radio and film to promote their artists. Nevertheless, although such reproductive media – including records themselves, of course – were necessary to attract the mass audience the industry needed, live performance continued to play a significant part in the process as well, being especially important for maintaining the aura of authenticity rock espoused. However, as the fiasco of the Beatles' concert at Shea Stadium in 1965 made clear, to produce spectacle on a grand scale would require vast improvements in lighting, amplification and logistics. The huge festivals of the late 1960s, Woodstock and Altamont, were essentially experiments. No one expected a peaceful assembly of 400,000 people at a farm in New York State, and no one foresaw the intense violence that erupted at Altamont Speedway in California later that same year. Whether an event succeeded or failed was more or less a matter of chance. To minimise risk and guarantee profit, it would be necessary to establish an efficient and stable apparatus. The activity of staging and promoting concerts would have to become more systematic.

Because any live gig happens in a particular place, all such performances could be described as site specific. Thus, many concert films are named after locations (Woodstock, the Isle of Wight). An audio-visual record of the performance, however, may remain more or less faithful to this specificity. Respecting the unity of time and place, the filmmaker risks boring the spectator with a canned performance (recall Kracauer's objections). As the title proclaims, the *mise-en-scène* of *Live at the Longhorn* is drawn exclusively from the Longhorn Ballroom, Dallas (as it existed on 10 January 1978).

Consider, for contrast, *Pink Floyd: Live at Pompeii* (Adrian Maben, 1972). Pink Floyd alongside the Sex Pistols? Nothing seems further from a concert by one of the archetypal dinosaur bands of rock than a show by the one of punk's progenitors. Pink Floyd's approach was polished and cerebral; the Sex Pistols' was raw and visceral. It is not surprising, then, that concert films of these bands should reflect these stylistic contrasts. One film captures Pink Floyd playing in an ancient arena with no audience present. The other features the Sex Pistols performing in a club in the US Deep South. Both documentaries employ the industry's technical resources, yet each achieves a different result: the Floyd film looks and sounds professional but contrived, whereas the Pistols' movie appears amateurish but genuine.

Vast differences aside, the titles of both films promise the spectator an audio-visual record of a 'live' performance. But this term carries very different meanings in each instance. For *Live at Pompeii*, director Adrian Maben placed Pink Floyd in an ancient amphitheatre with no audience present to disrupt the band's musical meanderings. Thus, there's really nothing 'live' about *Live at Pompeii*, which was designed to be seen exclusively by audiences absent from the time and place of the event's initial occurrence. Maben sought this isolation in an attempt to produce an 'anti-Woodstock', as a way to avoid making just another concert film. For Maben, audience reaction had become boring and predictable. This may have been true for a Pink Floyd show. In 1978, however, the audience at a punk show was anything but ceremonially staid and well-behaved. So, whereas Roger Waters recollects spitting on a fan who was attempting to climb onto the stage, when punk arrived, it was the audience that spat on the band. The spitting stopped when bands graduated to playing theatres, where the orchestra pit served as a demilitarised zone. It made storming the stage difficult as well.

Live at the Longhorn shows plenty of what might be called audience 'participation'. Fortunately, Warner Bros., the Pistols' US record label, dispatched a film crew equipped with three cameras to capture the carnival that winter night in Dallas. The resultant film shows spit and paper cups flying toward the stage. In those shots taken from the back of the hall, the band appears in the distance beyond a field of swaying arms – most extending a middle finger to the band. The view from the wings shows Sid Vicious giving a performance only marginally related to that of the rest of the band. At one point, a woman head-butts Sid forcefully enough to start blood flowing from his nose down his bare chest. One patron front and centre appears to be getting ready to urinate on the stage. Such antics were – and still are – *de rigueur* at punk shows. It is worth quoting Dick Hebdige at length:

> It was in the performance arena that punk groups posed the clearest threat to law and order. Certainly, they succeeded in subverting the conventions of concert and nightclub entertainment. Most significantly, they attempted both physically and in terms of lyrics and life-style to move closer to their audiences. This in itself is by no means unique: the boundary between artist and audience has often stood as a metaphor in revolutionary aesthetics (Brecht, the surrealists, Dada, Marcuse, etc.) for that larger and more intransigent life under capitalism. The stages of those venues secure enough to host 'new wave' acts were regularly invaded by hordes of punks, and if the management refused to tolerate such blatant disregard for ballroom etiquette, then the groups and their followers could be drawn closer together in a communion of spittle and mutual abuse. (1979: 110)

Employing a similarly sympathetic perspective, David James valorises this violation of the boundaries between performer and audience as 'the ritual passage of the audience over the stage and their playful contestation of the band's position on it and control over it'; for James, this transgression represents punk's 'alterity to corporate consumer culture' (1996: 225). Although his point is valid – these people do not passively consume the spectacle but take an active role in producing it – such transgression does not always remain 'playful' but often turns malevolent. During the Pistols' tour of the South, many paying customers came to the shows predisposed to hate the band and bent on doing mischief. Perhaps the musicians hoped naively that working class people like themselves would ultimately prove receptive to their music, but it is safe to say that their manager, Malcolm McLaren, expected – even hoped – reception to be hostile.

A live concert produces both musical and non-musical or extra-musical communications between performers and audience. The greatest part of these travel in a single direction only. Most often, extra-musical utterances broadcast from the stage command the audience to perform some regimented mass action such as clapping hands in time to the music. The performers, after all, have exclusive access to the public address (PA) system, and this situation establishes the performer as addressor and the audience as addressee, whose contribution is essentially limited to predictable responses such as clapping or singing along. Of course, it has become a cliché of the rock concert for the performer to aim the microphone at the audience, prompting them to sing a line or chorus. It would be a mistake, however, to regard this ritualistic ventriloquism as effecting even a temporary shift of power: the audience is simply reacting on cue. Obviously, the words they sing are not their own. As for solid bodies crossing boundaries, most of such instances are innocuous; for instance, a singer pulls a woman from the audience to dance with him. Even in the practice known as stage diving, audience members are more likely to injure themselves than the band. However, a body risks less harm in the mosh pit than on the stage, where the very apparatus that facilitates the musicians' visibility makes them easy targets. As noted above, the situation can become dangerous when missiles hurled from the environment breach the invisible membrane protecting the stage. This menace may explain why the industrial band Ministry chose to erect a chain link fence between itself and its audience for its 1989–90 tour. The motivation for such a structure differs from Pink Floyd's erecting a wall as performance. In *The Making of The Wall* documentary, Roger Waters describes how he envisioned a concert in which a wall would be built between the band and the audience. When the wall was finished, the concert would be over. Waters' idea suggests an interesting approach to musical duration and physical movement. The important point here, however, involves the irony of constructing a barrier between performers and audience. Of course, the image of a wall never signified positively in Pink Floyd's iconography; nevertheless, how strange to conceive of a concert in which communication between musicians and audience diminishes as the show proceeds.

A conventionally successful concert depends on establishing and maintaining the distinction between performance space and the rest of the room. To this end, the stage represents the most important instance of what Niklas Luhmann calls the 'special arrangements' that separate artistic performance from non-artistic objects and events (2000: 110). Although stars are marked as special even before they take the stage, it is nevertheless their presence on stage that confirms their difference from the punters. Thus, the logistics of stage construction are crucial. Note that Mel Stuart's documentary *Wattstax* (1973) begins with shots of the stage construction, represented as an organised and orderly job. Such images highlight the social significance of a large, peaceful gathering of black Americans in the heart of a troubled urban area. In contrast, the *ad hoc* construction at the Altamont Speedway in *Gimme Shelter* portended disaster, as noted in a previous chapter. Due to last minute changes of venue, the stage, located at the bottom of a hill, was built too low to contain the crowd adequately. Throughout the day, performances were continually disrupted by battles breaking out between Hells Angels and audience members around the lip of the stage. Putting aside the issues of *who* was responsible for asking the Hells Angels to participate and precisely *what* role they were asked to perform, we know for certain that their presence on stage was intended to shore up the porous boundary. The unintended consequence, however, was to blur the distinction between legitimate security and outlaw force. Such strategic alliances are typical if dangerous. They constitute what Deleuze and Guattari (1987) identify as the fragile treaty between the state and the nomadic war machine. (Thus, Sonny Barger's on-air disclaimer: 'I ain't no cop.' At least Barger understood the importance of maintaining the distinction between law and outlaw.) At one point, the film shows singer Marty Balin of Jefferson Airplane jumping off-stage to intervene in a brawl only to be knocked unconscious. Balin should have realised that, by abandoning his consecrated place above the fray, he forfeited his special status. When his band mate Paul Kantner uses the PA to blame the assault on the Angels, one of the club's members grabs a microphone to defend his brethren. A tense debate follows that could only have occurred because the boundary between system and environment had become so permeable. Later, after the fracas between the Angels and audience member Meredith Hunter, which resulted in the latter's death, Keith Richards uses the PA to issue an ultimatum to the Angels, whining into the microphone: 'If those cats don't stop beating everybody up in sight, we're splitting'. An Angel cuts him short to respond that Hunter had been spotted brandishing a gun. This information throws the situation into utter confusion. A high-angle shot of the stage shows clearly that, in terms of sheer numbers of bodies, the Stones have lost possession of that territory.

The relatively unfettered conditions of large outdoor festivals contrast greatly with the confinement of indoor shows, where the well-planned space of the theatre has replaced the free, unbounded space of the festival grounds. Deleuze and Guattari use the terms 'smooth' and 'striated' to describe, alternately, a place one occupies without measure (for example, the sea or desert) and a place thoroughly divided and apportioned (such as the Jeffersonian grid of the modern city). The authors go as far as to claim that architecture is allied with the state apparatus whereas music and drugs have an affinity with the nomadic war machine (1987: 402). Whereas the outdoor festival site conforms to the smooth space suited for free, nomadic movement, the tall stages, orchestra pits and neat rows of seats that characterise theatre architecture tend to impose order on events. In addition, the economics of graduated ticket pricing and assigned seating prohibit wandering about and adopting multiple perspectives. In such a truly sedentary environment, an usher shows you to your place, from which you can look forward and upwards towards the spectacle. The class politics of British punk guaranteed that unruly crowds would bristle at such control. *The Future is Unwritten* (2007), for instance, shows the Clash berating violent bouncers at a Glasgow show for their rough handling of the audience. Strummer's voice-over claims that the Clash 'were one with the audience'; unfortunately, that lofty sentiment hardly describes the actual state of affairs.

Unlike the situation in a theatre, however, nightclub stages need not conform to any standard or regulation regarding height. Each stage is unique to its venue: some rise a good five feet above floor level, while others stand barely a foot higher than the rest of the room. Differences of height aside, all function to delimit the performance space apart from that of spectatorship. As Wendy Fonarow notes about indie-band gigs: 'the line between audience and performer may be as thin as a piece of tape stuck to the floor' (1997: 361). It is crucial that the performance space is indicated or *marked* as such in opposition to the unmarked environment the audience inhabits.[9] Of course, factors other than stage construction function to distinguish the performance space. A powerful sound system ensures that the audible sound comes from the stage. The PA system broadcasts the performers' message to its audience. Stage lighting renders events in the performance area visible while low ambient lighting in the room signals the supposed insignificance of goings on there. Nevertheless, it is hardly the case that the audience pays solely to hear the music or see the musicians perform; many attend a show to observe or participate in a 'scene' event. But the effect of dimming the house lights restores primary collective focus on the stage performers.

Reinforcing this perspective, most concert movies position the camera as an omniscient spectator, whose view is consistently clear of bobbing heads and other distractions. The three cameras in the Pistols' film, however, never afford us this totalising, transcendent point-of-view (no 'God' shots). Never larger-than-life, the Pistols are represented in all-too-human scale. At times, the camera places us in the crowd; at other times, we get a view from the wings of the stage. Throughout, the camera remains solidly anchored on the floor. Yet, still, the filmmaker remains aloof from the crowd. Rothman correctly describes the situation when he remarks, 'the cinema-verité filmmaker withholds himself from the world in order to film it' (1996: 8). In the observational mode of filmmaking, the camera facilitates transcendence. To put it another way, the ability to distinguish between system and environment attributes to the observer a perspective limited to neither. The embodied observer cannot both occupy a place within the totality of the concert and simultaneously transcend that situation. Transcendence, however, implies rising above, whereas *distinction* simply means setting apart. In this instance, the practical decision to refuse to mount the camera on a crane repudiates the transcendent perspective.

THIS IS THE BERLIN WALL

For me, the climax of the show occurs during 'Holidays in the Sun'. Rotten introduces the song with the line, 'a cheap holiday in other people's misery'. The reference to a holiday invokes the Pistols' own brief exile in Berlin, where McClaren sent the band to cool their heels while the British public's rage against the band subsided. The song also documents a moment when economic conditions made visiting Germany a bargain for British tourists. Rotten attacks the perverse exploitation that treats Nazi death camps as theme parks. Yet if the lyrics Rotten sings transport spectators to the death camps and the Berlin Wall, they also insist on keeping before our eyes the spectacle taking place in the Longhorn Ballroom in January 1978. About halfway through the song, Rotten gestures toward the lip of the stage and declares, 'this is the Berlin Wall', drawing an analogy between the Iron Curtain and the stage proscenium. I want to unpack the metaphor of the wall as obstacle to social interaction and communication. Among the definitions of *wall* listed in the *Oxford English Dictionary*, we in fact find 'The Wall' as a reference to the Berlin Wall (def. 4h). As a common noun, the *O.E.D.* defines a *wall* as 'a rampart … constructed for defensive purposes'. It can also be an enclosing structure; that is, a wall contains the space within as it separates that space from the world outside. The scientific disciplines of anatomy, zoology and botany use the term wall to designate a cell membrane. In system's theory, the membrane is a necessary characteristic of an *autonomous* system, a system that is operationally closed.

Rotten declares his intention to 'go over the wall', an expression that means to defect or escape (*O.E.D.* III. 20). He is the one free to cross over, but he also invites the audience to join him and challenges them to tear down the boundary between performer and audience. He is also exhorting the latter to escape the oppression of a modern authoritarian state like the US, urging the rabble to storm the barricades, as it were. This apparent camaraderie is belied, however, by his confusing final request, 'Please don't be waiting for me', which Jon Savage calls 'one of the most terrifying admissions in all pop' (2001: 412). To whom does Rotten address this injunction?

When Rotten sings, 'I'm looking at them and they're looking at me', he points to the reciprocity that forms the essence of successful coupling between two autonomous systems. Yet, although Rotten acknowledges the reciprocal gaze between performer and spectator, he is aware that 'them and me' remain on different sides of the Wall. Rotten had already violated the distinction by bringing a fan into the band to play bass. As Dick Hebdige writes, Sid Vicious 'had made the symbolic crossing from the dance floor to the stage' (1979: 111). Unfortunately, the crossing would remain symbolic, as Sid never really learned to play the instrument. In fact, his presence on stage destroyed the band's musical unity. Worse still, the entire organisation that was 'The Sex Pistols' had nearly disintegrated by early 1978. Vicious and Rotten no longer spoke with their manager McLaren. Sid's drug habit had thoroughly alienated him from the rest of the band, including his former mate Rotten. Moreover, the latter saw himself as standing apart from journeymen musicians Jones and Cook, whom he increasingly treated as sidemen. Of course, the 'lead singer' in general is distinguished from the rest of the band simply by his or her front-and-centre position on stage. *Live at the Longhorn* does contain an oddly pathetic moment of camaraderie between Rotten and Jones. During one of the breaks between songs, Sid has fallen down and split his nose open. Looking towards Vicious, whom he mocks over the PA as 'a living circus', Rotten turns towards Jones and laughs.

Sid has made a spectacle of himself, but not, of course, for the first time on the tour. As raucous as *Live at the Longhorn* looks, it does not contain one of the most violent moments of punk performance captured on film. I refer to Sid Vicious clobbering members of the audience with his solid-body Fender bass. That scene, which occurred during the San Antonio concert two days before the Dallas gig, appears in Lech Kowalski's *D.O.A.* (1981). Although he is credited as director, Kowalski got his raw footage from a project begun by Tom Forcade, then publisher and editor of *High Times*, who attempted to film the Pistols' 1978 American tour. Denied official access by Pistols' road manager Noel Monk, Forcade stubbornly persisted in gathering footage wherever and whenever he could. Consequently, his film crew had the status of outsiders – a position they occupied literally, as security often chased them from the shows. Despite the obstacles to filming the gigs, *D.O.A.* contains a good deal of concert footage along with *vox pop* interviews with other outsiders such as frustrated ticket holders or troublemakers who have been expelled from the venue. The film in fact contains an interview with the man who provoked Vicious's assault.

Live at the Longhorn does leave a shockingly graphic audio-visual record of the Sex Pistols' bass player's deteriorating physical state. Vicious began the tour as an addict with no access to the kind of medical care that might mitigate the effects of heroin withdrawal. The situation was complicated by the bodyguards Noel Monk assigned to watch over Vicious and isolate him from undesirable influences (i.e. heroin). While such vigilant surveillance kept Vicious out of trouble (somewhat), it left him no opportunities to score drugs. As the tour progressed from Atlanta through Memphis, Austin, San Antonio and Baton Rouge, Vicious was barely able to stave off sickness with pills and alcohol, always teetering on the verge of collapse. By the time the band reached Dallas, he was desperate to score.

Scoring heroin involves an elaborate communication ritual between addicts and dope peddlers that begins with recognition and attraction, and develops into a complicated coupling that oscillates between trust and suspicion. On a concert tour, however, constant traveling over long distances allows no time for the extended courtship between junkie and pusher to develop. A stranger in every city the band played and dogged by Monk's men, Vicious

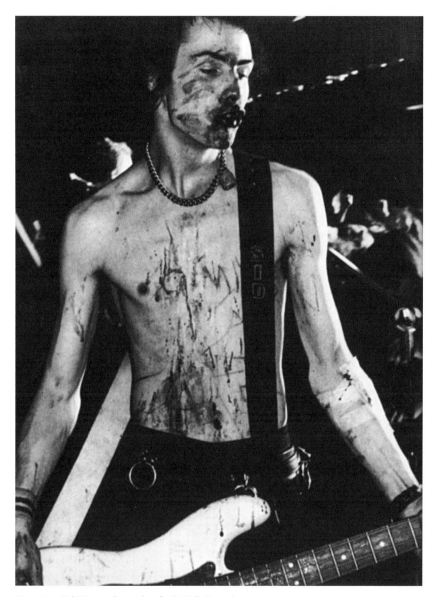

Figure 7 – Sid Vicious demands a fix (© Bob Gruen)

had to revert to more direct advertising. His solution can be seen in one of the more infamous images taken during the Dallas show. Instead of making a verbal plea for junk, Sid has literally etched the words 'GIMME A FIX' into his chest with a knife. This gruesome message serves to broadcast his addiction, as if the body itself were trying to bypass speech and communicate its needs directly. Sending out a plea by writing on the body both demonstrates and undermines the very notion of writing, which implies the absence of addressor and addressee. The message cut into Sid's chest produces an interesting communication situation because, to respond appropriately to the message, the interlocutor must be in the sender's presence. Certainly, I can read this text years after it was written, on a body long dead. As such, it functions as a historical document testifying to Sid's addiction. But the message will have failed to produce the desired effect unless sender and receiver occupy a common environment.

Jean-Francois Lyotard (1988) has argued that, given the occurrence of a phrase/sentence, another phrase/sentence *must* follow. Of course, not just any phrase will win the stakes. There is an art to joining phrases, which coexist in a common phrase universe. The genre of discourse provides the test of appropriateness. In the present instance, the discourse of entreaty cannot work without the proximity of two physical beings. A body can only fix if a needle breaks skin, a result that would effect the structural coupling (body and drug) that allows Sid to survive (until, ironically, he overdoses). In this communicative exchange, the stakes depend on a successful transaction of drugs for words. The appropriate response for this genre of discourse is a shot of heroin.

A verbal phrase may be followed by a physical response. Punk rockers wore charged and abrasive slogans and icons on their clothes to invite a reaction, which could never be calculated precisely. A confrontational move might backfire and provoke even greater aggression from the offended party. Under ideal conditions, the appropriate answer to a phrase should be another phrase, but both interlocutors must be bound by the rules of that genre of discourse called argumentation or debate. Ironically, the very institutions punk attacked were responsible for safeguarding those rules. Following the success of the 'God Save the Queen' single, Lydon had been assaulted by an armed mob and was seriously injured. The gauntlet was thrown down not only over politics but also over musical taste. Wearing a 'Pink Floyd Sucks' t-shirt not only set oneself apart from the status quo but also drew a line in the sand to test the enemy's nerve or mettle. Retaliation varied according to the different tribes that formed youth subcultures in 1970s England. Challenging laid-back hippies involved little risk, but insulting a bunch of Teddy Boys had serious consequences. An offense could take the form of simply not respecting a distinction manifest as sartorial style. For instance, Paul Cook recalls being beaten up by a bunch of Teddy Boys for wearing Ted shoes in public (see Savage 2001: 366).

The danger of pulling down the barricades emerges during the band's encore of 'No Fun' in Dallas. An encore is itself an ambiguous supplement that simultaneously belongs within the show's limits yet, strictly speaking, remains outside those bounds. In this final opportunity to break the boundaries that have kept participants in the concert event apart, decorum gives way to carnival. These enthusiastic eruptions of 'spontaneous' appreciation had quickly reified into predictable behaviour at rock concerts. Throughout the 1970s, as the live rock concert became an institution, what was once reserved for extraordinary occasions became a *de rigueur* part of the ritual, and this rock cliché must have bored and angered Rotten. 'More of us?' he taunts the crowd, 'You must be mad!' The singer has changed clothes and is now sporting a black torn T-shirt adorned with skull and crossbones. Pinned on his collar is a black Swastika set in a bright red circle. The fascination with Nazi iconography was a fundamental reason why Bernie Rhodes had split from McLaren and the Pistols. I doubt if Rotten fully understood how juxtaposing these images flattened the distinction between mock violence and real-world genocide.

Live at the Longhorn exhibits some masterful editing of an unfolding battle over stage territory. We see close-ups of Jones's face, but no matching shot reveals the object of his gaze. Still, Jones is obviously angry with someone. He lunges at the audience with the neck of his guitar, then stops playing to strike out with his fist. Fortunately, the altercation is broken up by Noel Monk, whose admonishments appear to tame the offending culprit. The film cuts to a shot from behind the Pistols of an audience member who seems to be unzipping his jeans. Cut to another close-up of Jones, who is wearing an expression of sober resignation and shaking his head in disbelief.

By now, the audience has taken possession of the front of the stage, forcing Rotten and Vicious onto the drum riser. We get a telling shot from stage right of Rotten and Jones, the former frantically screaming into the microphone and the latter looking bored and resigned, simply nodding his head in time to the music. This is clearly 'no fun' for the guitarist, who, along with drummer Paul Cook, had aspired to more conventional pop stardom rather than the notoriety the Pistols achieved. Suddenly, Rotten's manic assault abruptly ceases. This schizoid transformation from raving demon to dazed onlooker was typical of Rotten's performances during his (initial) Sex Pistols period. From his vantage point atop the drum riser, and shielding his eyes with his hand, he calmly surveys the chaos. It is worth recalling that the Pistols are covering a song by Iggy and the Stooges. Unlike Rotten, Iggy Pop has consistently courted bodily danger by diving into the audience or inviting the latter on stage. Iggy's visceral performances contrast sharply with Rotten's cold-blooded stare. The British singer has shifted from engaged participant to detached observer. As such, Rotten is the very symbol of Punk's despair as it confronted its own failure to tear down the monuments of rock's past. Of course, change implies not only negating the past but setting forth a new state of affairs. This would naturally prove difficult for a movement that reveled in its lack of a future. Less than a week after the Dallas show, the Pistols played a final disastrous gig in San Francisco and split up (for thirty years!).[10] Something akin to punk (i.e. *hard core*) subsequently emerged on the west coast of the US, with bands like the Dead Kennedys and Black Flag.[11] Yet, despite stylistic similarities to the British brand, punk had metamorphosed into something other.

NOTES

1   In order to thrive, the popular music industry needs a continual supply of both rock stars for sale and fans to buy that product. To sustain the hyperactive metabolism of this organism/organisation, select recruits from a current generation of fans routinely rise to become tomorrow's stars. In the 1970s, this system had come to resemble a craft guild, with fledgling rockers paying their dues in clubs and bars to gain all-important *credentials*.

2   Another recent offering is *Never Mind the Sex Pistols: An Alternative History* (2007), made by Alan Parker (a.k.a. 'Mr. Punk') for Channel 4. Parker's *Who Killed Nancy?* (2009) employs numerous interviews and examines police records to vindicate Vicious of his girlfriend's murder.

3   Kowalski, too, has acquired a certain cult status as filmmaker, creating excellent documentaries on Dee Dee Ramone (*Hey, Is Dee Dee Home?* [2002]) and Johnny Thunders (*Born to Lose* [1999]), as well as the semi-documentary featuring John Spacely, *Gringo, Story of a Junkie* (1987). Working as both a Hollywood industry insider and an outsider, Penelope Spheeris followed *The Decline of Western Civilization* with *The Decline of Civilization Part II: The Metal Years* (1988). Amos Poe went on to make feature films, including *Alphabet City* (1984) and a remake of Andy Warhol's *Empire* (*Empire II* [2007]).

4   Credit information is minimal and hard to find. The DVD copy I worked from lists Lydon's manager Eric Gardner as executive producer along with Anita Camarata. Special thanks is extended to Bob Regehr, who worked for Warner Bros. and was instrumental in signing the Pistols.

5   *The Tree of Knowledge* (1998) contains a good popularisation of Maturana and Varela's theory.

6   See, for example, the numerous texts authored by Luhmann on a variety of topics.

7   For example, for the Rolling Stones, Ron Wood replaced Mick Taylor, who replaced Brian Jones. Although instrumentalists are more than expendable than lead singers, even the latter can be replaced. But Ronnie Biggs, the famous train robber Malcolm McLaren hoped would keep the Pistols going, was no Johnny Rotten.

8   Today, Lydon's cynicism sounds hollow in the light of the inclusion of a pair of Sex Pistols' songs on *Guitar Hero III*.

9   John E. Kaemmer, following folklorist Richard Bauman, claims performances are distinctive events because they are intended for an audience's evaluation. They are marked as special: 'In the Western world the concert setting often serves as a marker, including special dress or costumes, the dimming lights, the applause and the bow' (1993: 17). As Kaemmer points out, these accoutrements often have no direct bearing on the sound produced.

10 In early 1979, Sid Vicious was charged with murdering his girlfriend and subsequently died from a heroin overdose. The reunion tour featured original Pistols' bassist Glenn Matlock.

11 Many films have appeared that chronicle the Los Angeles and San Francisco scenes. The only film, however, that captures the aggressively violent yet ecstatic energy of the performances is Spheeris' *Decline of Western Civilization*.

CONCLUSION: SIMPLE GESTURES AND SMOOTH SURFACES IN ROBERT CAHEN'S *BOULEZ-RÉPONS*

Music often carries me away like a sea

– Charles Baudelaire, La Musique (1964: 93)

I began this study by suggesting that performance might offer a concrete way to conceive of the relation between musical motion and moving images. To support this claim, I contrasted relatively unembellished representations of human physical gesture with the baroque abstractions typical of 'visual music' animation. This might seem to imply that nothing could be further from avant-garde experimentation than the prosaic depiction of musical performance. Such a (mistaken) conclusion is promoted by Kracauer's critical attack on films that feature musical performances: as we recall, he dismisses the entire genre as necessarily uncinematic. Furthermore, various documentary film-makers have echoed Kracauer's objections, lamenting the inevitable sameness of musical performance documentaries imposed by the (perceived) limitations of the form. However, I want to emphasise that no absolute injunction exists against mixing realist representation with abstract experimentation. In this final chapter, I examine the successful confluence of visual and sonic experimentation in Robert Cahen's videotape of a performance of Pierre Boulez's challenging composition *Répons* (*Boulez-Répons* (1985)).

Though less well-known than 'star' video artists Bill Viola or Gary Hill, Cahen nevertheless possesses a considerable reputation in the field. Since the early 1970s, he has produced an impressive body of film and video work. Like Viola and Hill, he draws on the structural principles of music for inspiration. Sandra Lischi, the foremost scholar on Cahen, has even described his work as 'visible music', and her monograph on the director introduces him as 'a musician who adopts a poetic approach to images' (1997: 6). Indeed, music and poetry embrace the repetitions that story forms like the realist novel and classical Hollywood film must avoid in order to maintain their linear narrative drive. I prefer to point to this fascination with repetitive structure to explain the close relation between video art and experimental music. Although some have suggested that the process of working with tape (video and audio) unites the two arts in a single medium (see Meigh-Andrews 2006), cutting audio tape hardly resembles video editing.

Still, it is true that Cahen began writing music by manipulating sounds on audiotape. This manner of composing suited Cahen, who had no formal musical training. This technique, known as *musique concrete*, Cahen learned from Pierre Schaeffer, with whom he studied at the Groupe de Recherche Musicale. For a period, Cahen worked in the documentary unit at ORTF, France's television station, but his enthusiasm soon waned for conventional 'informational' video (see Lischi 1997: 13).[1] Despite Cahen's training in television documentary production, *Boulez-Répons* bears little resemblance to the typical concert documentary. As Lischi observes, 'Cahen's visualisation of a concert has nothing in common with conventional TV broadcasts' (1997: 59).

Nevertheless, the distinct documentary flavour of *Boulez-Répons* affords it a peculiar place in Cahen's *oeuvre*. In spite of its liberal use of visual special effects such as slow motion, superimposition and mirror imagery,[2] it contains segments of straightforward performance footage shot during an orchestra rehearsal at the Centre Pompidou. As a consequence, it appeals to a diverse if small audience. That is, it should interest fans and students of Boulez's music as well as people curious about Cahen's video art. Moreover, as time passes, the video will accrue documentary value. For it not only represents a performance of a modern musical masterpiece but also provides an audio-visual record of Boulez's practice as a conductor. Happily, the potential documentary riches do not come at the price of visually compelling imagery.

COUNTING TIME

An obsession with time constitutes the most pervasive theme throughout Cahen's work in general. In fact, Lischi has referred to him as 'a master of time', and she calls *Boulez-Répons* a piece that attempts 'to render time visible' (1997: 54). While this claim certainly holds true, I would like to discuss how Cahen treats space as well as time in his video. Although T. S. Eliot famously claimed that 'music moves only in time' (1971: 121), music, as organised sound, exists in space as well, and Boulez's composition utilises space in a very unusual way.[3]

For *Répons*, Boulez deploys musicians and electronic equipment in a unique spatial configuration. In fact, the work does not lend itself to performance in a conventional auditorium, in which the musicians on stage perform for an audience seated in ordered rows. On the contrary, it works best in a large venue such as a gymnasium, where reception can benefit from the increased distance between sound sources and audience. It is unfortunate that, considering how much thought Boulez has devoted to the relation of musicians to audience, no audience was present for the shooting of Cahen's video.[4] Boulez has distributed the instrumentalists and amplification equipment throughout the room so sounds might originate from any direction and then reverberate off of the walls, floor and ceiling, placing listeners deep within the sonic environment. Such a situation contrasts starkly with the traditional concert hall in which the music hails listeners from a relatively uniform direction. The physical arrangement of musicians for *Répons* is as follows. In the centre of the performance space, Boulez places the conductor's rostrum and a 24-piece chamber orchestra. The sounds produced by these acoustic instruments remain unamplified and unprocessed by the electronics. Surrounding this group of musicians, the audience would sit in a circle, and just beyond this area, six soloists comprise yet another outer ring. These soloists play percussive instruments: harp, piano, organ, cymbalum, vibraphone, xylophone, glockenspiel. The sounds produced by these are subjected to real-time electronic processing utilising the 4X, a powerful computer system developed at IRCAM under Boulez's guidance.[5] These digitally manipulated sounds are relayed by six loudspeakers mounted on the walls.

Cahen organised his video to follow the section divisions of *Répons*: 1. Instrumental introduction; 2. Entrance of soloists; 3. Alternation between soloists and orchestra; 4. Balinese passage; 5. Funeral march; 6. Rainy music; 7. Section built around repetition of notes; 8. Renewed alternation between soloists and orchestra (see Lischi 1997: 58). Viewers may have difficulty apprehending these divisions, however. More immediately striking is the gradual introduction of external imagery and the increasing real-time synchronisation of human gesture and resulting sound.

Figure 8 – Pierre Boulez beating time; Robert Cahen, *Boulez-Répons*, 1985. Courtesy Electronic Arts Intermix (EAI), New York.

Cahen's video begins with a medium close-up of the conductor in isolation, framed by a hazy white iris. A large speaker hangs on the wall behind his head. We see the partially obscured figure of a harpist sitting behind the conductor. The peculiar arrangement of performers for *Répons* means that Boulez faces only the chamber ensemble, making it difficult to communicate with the soloists positioned to his rear and sides. Boulez, whose gestures are consistently rendered in real time, conducts in a rather traditional style here, providing entrance cues to the players and beating time. In contrast to the conductor's synchronised movements, however, the musicians are depicted in slow motion – at first, even exclusively so, although, as Lischi notes, their gestures too will eventually be synchronised with the music (1997: 60).

About seven minutes into the piece, the camera shows a high-angle shot of the ensemble and tracks back to give us our first establishing shot of the performance space. We see the ensemble seated on a slightly raised platform and the conductor standing at his rostrum. At his back are the audio technicians who control the computers and mixing boards that route the sounds to the amplification and processing equipment. To the rear of the frame, we can see the pianist seated at his instrument. At this point, Cahen introduces the water imagery that provides a major visual theme in the video. Following a close-up of the mixing desk and a pair of unprocessed shots of the xylophonist and the pianist, the waves reappear to fill most of the frame, leaving only the bottom right corner for the technicians and their machines – tiny figures that occupy modest territory in proportion to the immense roiling sea that threatens to overwhelm them.

Cahen has chosen these liquid images to express a sympathy with Boulez's music. Such attempts to embody the mental pictures risk trivialising the music.[6] The water imagery might be read simply as a rendering of the undulating waves of sound. I fear, however, that such a literal reading of audio-visual correspondences forces a programmatic meaning on the sounds and mistakenly treats the composition as an instance of tone painting. Instead, I prefer to interpret the sounds and images as commentary on space. Employing video keying effects, Cahen has introduced images of water, forest and sky within the starkly modernist confines of the Centre Pompidou. These are more than just random images of nature.

Here we might recall Deleuze and Guattari's distinction between smooth and striated space broached in the previous chapter. The authors cite both maritime and musical instances, referring to the sea as the archetype of smooth space (1987: 480). It is quite apposite to invoke this distinction between smooth and striated space, for Deleuze and Guattari borrowed the concept from Boulez himself (see Boulez 1971). The composer invokes it to explain modern music's tendency to transcend the system of tempered tuning that divides an octave into twelve equal units. Boulez's own career path has taken him from the rigid mathematical formulae of serial composition towards an exploration of the upper limits of the overtone series where 'the ear will lose all landmarks and all absolute cognizance of intervals'. The sounds Boulez describes would resemble the glissando typical of sirens. Boulez goes on to claim that 'this is comparable to the eye's inability to estimate distances on a perfectly smooth surface' (1971: 85). In other words, he compares the ear's disorientation with the eye's loss of a vanishing point on the horizon. Listening to *Répons*, one loses one's bearings and drifts through a sonic environment of indistinct pitches. Cahen has rendered a visual analogue to this world, where the viewer often loses their sense of place *vis-à-vis* on-screen space. This disorientation is accomplished through a plethora of unsettling visual effects, including tight framings, densely superimposed images and split-screens. Yet, despite Cahen's penchant for abstraction, numerous shots of the musicians performing in real time continually reaffirm the world of ordinary perception. (In fact, certain shots of the soloists appear prosaic enough to make one conjure up the spectre of a gloating Kracauer, shaking his head disapprovingly.)

Besides introducing images of landscape and seascape into the narrowly bounded world of the performance space, Cahen also employs shots of theatre artist and dancer Hideyuki Yano running in slow motion, a figure that recurs throughout the piece. The precise motivation for this image seems rather puzzling. I suggest, however, that the pace of Yano's running functions like a clock against which other tempos might be measured. In the process of running, the regular alternating motion of the legs works like the tick/tock of the clock, each step the same yet different. Most important is the connection between Yano's legs and Boulez's arms as they beat time: each of these repetitive motions indicates tempo. The alternating movement of running recalls the birth of modern conducting in the Renaissance choir master's *tactus*, which originally consisted of two strokes of the arm: one up, one down (see Houle 1987). Such practices effectively measure the passing of time according to space covered through bodily locomotion. As such, they are quite opposed to actual duration and smooth space.

SIMPLE GESTURES

In *Cinema 1: The Movement-Image*, Deleuze borrows Henri Bergson's notion of duration (*durée*) to forge his argument on cinematic motion (1986: 7–11). In *Creative Evolution*, Bergson opposes actual duration to abstract clock time, and he does so by invoking the example of the cinematograph (1944: 331–2). We are aware, of course, that film constructs the illusion of motion from a series of still frames (photographs or drawings) that travel through the camera and projector at a fixed pace (expressed as the ratio of frames per second). This technology entails important consequences regarding time and motion. First, by dividing movement into a series of equidistant immobile sections, the cinema fails to capture movement's fluid and indivisible essence. Second, cinema presents time as a succession of unexceptional instants rather than as a collection of privileged moments resulting in ideal poses (Deleuze 1986: 4). Whereas ancient art strove to represent kinesis through perfect forms, the cinematograph introduced a radically new mode of representing motion, extracting the extraordinary from a parade of unexceptional instants. However, this is not how conducting works in general, and it is certainly not representative of Boulez's style of conducting in *Boulez-Répons*.

According to Boulez, the conductor should cultivate 'simple and directional' gestures to communicate with the orchestra. It is good practice to avoid movements that appear either 'too complicated' or that occur 'in a sort of abstract space' (2003: 102).[7] Movement must happen in a well-defined area circumscribed by the reach of the conductor's extended limbs. Within this area, and within the context of a specific gestural sign, certain points have significance for the musicians while others do not. For example, the vertical gesture that signals a downbeat begins at a certain point and stops at another. As with any language, these articulations are marked. Between these two poles lie uncountable undifferentiated (linguistically unmarked) points. The rather vague action of the conductor effects an amazing synchronicity, as the musicians must begin their attack at the precise instant when the conductor's arm comes to halt. The latter certainly qualifies as a privileged instant or pose; it is not derived from a set of 'any-instants-whatsoever'. In many ways, conducting an orchestra resembles nothing so much as playing the air guitar, except, of course, air guitarists do not cause the sounds they imitate. Still, such performances alternate stretches of frantic activity with conventional 'ideal' poses much like conducting.[8]

In Cahen's tape, Boulez performs an awkward ballet comprised of graceful choreography punctuated by mechanical jerks and grotesque poses. To a great degree, it is the spatial layout of musicians for *Répons* that causes Boulez to alternate between metrical conducting and a more fluid style. The composer has made the following observations on the difficulty in conducting the piece:

the soloists are conducted for most of the time by gestures that don't relate to tempo, while the orchestra in the centre is for the most part conducted metrically. Metrical conducting can also be applied to the soloists, but in this case the tempo will be inevitably slow, because, with the distance that separates me from the soloists, the beat cannot be too irregular or fast, otherwise the orchestral players will not have time to adapt simultaneously to reading the score and following the conductor. (2003: 103-4)

This delay results in a 'sonic shimmering' that Boulez describes as having a desirable 'stroboscopic' effect (2003: 106). We observe, then, Boulez's keen awareness of 'having to compose for a space in which some players are near the centre, and others further away' (2003: 105). He has carefully considered the role space plays in composition and performance.

In effect, Boulez has addressed the problem of how distance affects the relation between an initiating gesture and the sound it produces. Despite his comment that a conductor 'must really be able to "touch" the players, exactly as if they were the keys of a keyboard' (2003: 98), the presence of the scare quotes around the word 'touch' confirms that Boulez is speaking metaphorically. For, unlike other musicians, a conductor never makes actual contact with the surface of the instruments he or she plays. We have noted this phenomenon before, in the chapter on British documentary. However, perhaps no film we have encountered previously foregrounds the relation between physical gesture and the resulting musical sound so well as Cahen's video. Moreover, it does so by highlighting the absence of a visible material medium between the (conductor's) will and the act (of the musicians commanded to play). Conducting a musical ensemble involves even less contact between gesture and vibrating sound medium than, for example, playing the theremin. Perhaps an analogous musical performance would be Alvin Lucier's *Music for Solo Performer* (1964), which appears in an episode of Robert Ashley's video series *Music with its Roots in the Aether*. Via electroencephalography (EEG) technology, Lucier uses brainwaves to cause the membranes and metal surfaces of various percussion instruments to vibrate without touching them with either his hands or feet. The startling effect of such a performance depends on the seated performer keeping uncannily still. However, Lucier's piece raises different issues than Boulez's, virtually doing away with visible gesture. If an analogy exists between the two pieces, it would be in the electronic processing of waves (brain waves and sound waves).

In *Répons*, this digital audio processing plays an important role in overcoming the limitations of Western musical instruments. As *Répons* builds in intensity, audio phase shifting blurs the clarity of the individual notes that comprise the cascading chromatic passages. After all, the modern tempered keyboard represents the ultimate striated surface, dividing the sound continuum into discrete and equal units. For Boulez, equal temperament presents an obstacle to the smooth surfaces he seeks.

We might conclude by considering the reverse side of the complaint over the pedestrian predictability of most concert films. The fact is that avant-garde visual experiments are likely to annoy many fans who prefer straightforward images of their favorite musical celebrities. Is there no transcending this time-worn dilemma? Even in our postmodern age, modernist distinctions between mass culture and the avant-garde persist. On one hand, the music industry continues to manufacture undistinguished concert films designed to promote their product. On the other hand, there exists a much smaller body of audio-visual art works that welcomes the challenges of representing musical performance. It is not, I hope, merely false optimism to hope that the latter will continue to thrive. Whereas truly independent film and video are readily available only to an elite who live in metropolitan areas, the distribution of music through broadcast media has contributed to a more catholic and diverse musical taste. It would not be too difficult, I believe, to find a sizeable if geographically scattered public who appreciate the work of Fred Frith, Diamanda Galas or Meredith Monk. Because these artists are visually striking performers as well as innovative musicians, their talents shine brightest through audio-visual media. This situation bodes well for future projects that combine new music with equally challenging visual art.

NOTES

1   It is worth noting that both Cahen and Boulez have been employed by the state: Cahen with ORTF and later with Institut National de l'Audiovisuel (INA); Boulez as head of IRCAM. If we treat this video as a documentary, we might ask who is speaking here? Is it an institution or an individual? INA, IRCAM, Cahen, or Boulez?

2   Indeed, according to Lischi, *Boulez-Répons* boasts the most special effects of all Cahen's works (1997: 60).

3   Another noteworthy film dedicated to exploring how architectural space affects musical performance is *Sound of the Carceri* (François Girard, 1998). The film features cellist Yo-Yo Ma performing Bach in virtual environments constructed according to drawings by Giovanni Piranesi.

4   This absence condemns the piece to a certain artificiality and sterility (recall Pink Floyd in Pompeii). Cahen has not videotaped a 'concert' but a rehearsal.

5   A proponent of computer music, Boulez advocates real-time processing of audio in performances. He in fact has described the need to rely on pre-recorded material as 'unremitting torture' (2003: 85). On IRCAM, Boulez and the 4X, see Georgina Born's 1995 study.

6   Note Douglas Kahn's clever comment on the banality of this connection: 'There was water water everywhere in program music, but no one got wet' (1999: 245).

7   The final segment of the admittedly pedestrian *Of Men and Music* contains a portrait of conductor Dimitri Mitropoulos directed by Alexander 'Sasha' Hammid, famous for his collaboration with Maya Deren on *Meshes of the Afternoon* (1943). Hammid shows Mitropoulos conducting the New York Philharmonic rehearsing Lizst's *Faust Symphony*. Mitropoulos possessed an unorthodox style. He refused to use a baton and did not refer to the printed score while conducting. Contrast his supple and expressive hand and arm movements with Boulez's severe style.

8   See Alexander Lipsitz's rockumentary *Air Guitar Nation* (2006).

Bibliography

Ake, D. (2002) *Jazz Cultures*. Berkeley: University of California Press.

Allen, R. C. and D. Gomery (1985) *Film History: Theory and Practice*. New York: McGraw Hill.

Altman, R. (2004) *Silent Film Sound*. New York: Columbia University Press.

Anderson, T. (2006) *Making Easy Listening: Material Culture and Postwar American Recording*. Minneapolis: Minnesota University Press.

Anon. (2004) 'Heavy Metal Therapy: Interview with Joe Berlinger and Bruce Sinofsky', *Filmmaker*, summer 2004. Available at: http://www.filmmakermagazine.com/issues/summer2004/features/heavy_metal.php (accessed 27 November 2011).

____ (2006) 'DVD Consumer Sales, Week ending June 18', *Hollywood Reporter*. Available at: www.hollywoodreporter.com/tech (accessed 23 November 2011).

Appel, A. (1960) 'Jazz on a Summer's Day', *Film Quarterly*, 14, 1, Autumn, i–ii.

Aristotle (1936) *On the Soul*. Trans. W. S. Hett. Cambridge: Harvard University Press.

Arnheim, R. (1957) *Film as Art*. Berkeley: University of California Press.

Attali, J. (1992) *Noise: The Political Economy of Music*. Trans. B. Massumi. Minneapolis: University of Minnesota Press.

Auslander, P. (1999) *Liveness: Performance in a Mediatized Culture*. New York: Routledge.

____ (2006) *Performing Glam Rock: Gender and Theatricality in Popular Music*. Ann Arbor: University of Michigan Press.

Baily, J. (1985) 'Music Structure and Human Movement', in P. Howell, I. Cross and R. West (eds) *Musical Structure and Cognition*. London: Academic Press, 237–58.

Bailey, D. (1992) *Improvisation: Its Nature and Practice in Music*. New York: Da Capo.

Balazs, B. (1970) *Theory of the Film: Character and Growth of a New Art*. Trans. E. Bone. New York: Dover Publications.

Bangs, L. (2003) *Psychotic Reactions and Carburetor Dung*. Ed. G. Marcus. New York: Anchor.

Baraka, I. A. (1963) *Blues People: Negro Music in White America*. New York: William Morrow.

____ (2009) *Diggin': The Afro-American Soul of American Classical Music*. Berkeley:

University of California Press.

Barger, R. 'Sonny' (2001) *Hell's Angel*. New York: Harper Collins.

Barnouw, E. (1974) *Documentary: A History of the Non-Fiction Film*. New York: Oxford University Press.

Barsam, R. M. (1992) *Non-Fiction Film: A Critical History*. Bloomington: Indiana University Press.

Barthes, R. (1972) 'The Face of Garbo', in *Mythologies*. Trans. A. Lavers. New York: Hill and Wang, 56–7.

_____ (1985) 'Musica Practica', in *The Responsibility of Forms*. Trans. R. Howard. Berkeley: University of California Press, 261–6.

Bataille, G. (1985) 'The Jesuve', in A. Stoekl (ed.) *Visions of Excess: Selected Writings 1927–1939*. Trans. A. Stoekl, C. R. Lovett and D. M. Leslie. Minneapolis: University of Minnesota Press, 73–8.

Baudelaire, C. (1964) 'La Musique', in *Baudelaire: Selected Verse*. Trans. Francis Scarfe. Baltimore: Penguin, 93-94.

Bazin, A. (1972) *What is Cinema? vol II*. Trans. H. Gray. Berkeley: University of California Press.

Beattie, K. (2008) *Documentary Display: Re-Viewing Nonfiction Film and Video*. London: Wallflower Press.

Bebb, B. (1982) 'The Cool Medium of Shirley Clarke', *The Los Angeles Weekly Reader*, 26 February, 1–2, 16.

Benjamin, W. (1968) *Illuminations*. Trans. H. Zohn. H. Arendt (ed.). New York: Schocken.

Berg, C. M. (1978) 'Cinema Sings the Blues', *Cinema Journal*, 17, 2, 1–12.

Bergman, G. (2000) 'Gimme Shelter: Snapshots from the Road'. Available at: http://www.criterion.com/current/posts/105-gimme-shelter-snapshots-from-the-road (accessed 28 November 2011).

Bergson, H. (1944) *Creative Evolution*. Trans. A. Mitchell. New York: Modern Library.

Blakeston, O. (1928) 'Disconnected Thoughts on Music and the Cinema', *Close Up*, 3, 39–43.

Blacking, J. (1973) *How Musical is Man?* Seattle: University of Washington Press.

Bluem, A. W. (1977) *Documentary in American Television: Form, Function, Method*. New York: Hastings House.

Boden, M. A. (2003) *The Creative Mind: Myths and Mechanisms*. London: Basic.

Bohen, F. M. and A. Westin (1968) Letter to Shirley Clarke. 16 October. Shirley Clarke Papers, archives of the University of Wisconsin.

Booth, S. (1984) *The True Adventures of the Rolling Stones*. New York: Vintage.

Bordwell, D. (2005) *Figures Traced in Light: On Cinematic Staging*. Berkeley: University of California Press.

Born, G. (1995) *Rationalizing Culture: IRCAM, Boulez, and the Institutionalization of the Musical Avant-Garde*. Berkeley: University of California Press.

Boulez, P. (1971) *Boulez on Music Today*. Trans. S. Bradshaw and R. R. Bennett.

Cambridge: Harvard University Press.

_____ (2003) *On Conducting*. London: Faber and Faber.

Bourdieu, P. (1984) *Distinction: A Social Critique of the Judgement of Taste*. Trans. R. Nice. Cambridge, MA: Harvard University Press.

Bowser, E. (1990) *The Transformation of Cinema: 1907–1915*. Berkeley: University of California Press.

Boyle, D. (1986) *Video Classics: A Guide to Video Art and Documentary Tapes*. Phoenix: Oryx Press.

Bresson, R. (1975) *Notes on the Cinematographer*. Trans. J. Griffin. Los Angeles: Green Integer.

Britt, S. (1989) *Dexter Gordon: A Musical Biography*. New York: Da Capo.

Burch, N. (1990) *Life to Those Shadows*. Ed. and Trans. B. Brewster. Berkeley: University of California Press.

Chanan, M. (2007) *The Politics of Documentary*. London: British Film Institute.

Chion, M. (1994) *Audio-vision: Sound on Screen*. Trans. C. Gorbman. New York: Columbia University Press.

Christgau, R. (1969) 'Anatomy of a Love Festival', *Robert Christgau: Dean of American Rock Critics*. Available at: www.robertchristgau.com/xg/music/monterey-69.php. (accessed 22 February 2010).

Clarke, S. (n.d.) unpublished notebook, Shirley Clarke Papers, archives of the University of Wisconsin.

_____ (1968) 'A Proposal to Do a Film on Jazz Composer Ornette Coleman', Shirley Clarke Papers, archives of the University of Wisconsin.

_____ (1968) Letter to Humphrey Burton. Archives of the University of Wisconsin.

Cohen, T. F. (2001) 'How Cinema Changes Music: Metronomes, Maestros, and Musical Composition', unpublished PhD thesis, University of Florida.

Conley, T. (2005) 'Faciality', in *The Deleuze Dictionary*. Ed. A. Parr. New York: Columbia University Press, 96–8.

Cross, I. (2003) 'Music as a Biocultural Phenomenon', in G. Avanzini, C. Faienza, D. Minciacchi, L. Lopez and M. Majno (eds) *The Neurosciences and Music*. New York: New York Academy of Sciences, 106–11.

Crouch, S. (1998) 'Bird Land', in C. Woideck (ed.) *Charlie Parker Companion: Six Decades of Commentary*. New York: Schirmer, 251–62.

Crowdus, G. and R. Porton (2006) 'The Great Pretender: An Interview with Willem Dafoe', *Cineaste*, 31, 40–7.

Crowther, B. (1951) '"Of Men and Music", in Which Leading Artists Display Their Talents', *New York Times*, 15 February. Available at: http://movies.nytimes.com/movie/review?res=9403DD138E13BBC4D52DFB466838A64 (accessed 9 January 2009).

Dahl, L. (1999) *Morning Glory: A Biography of Mary Lou Williams*. Berkeley: University of California Press.

Dalcroze, E. (1988) *Rhythm, Music, and Education*. Trans. H. F. Rubinstein. Salem, MA: Aver Company Publishers.

Darwin, C. (1965) *The Expression of the Emotions in Man and Animals*. Chicago: University of Chicago Press.

Davidson, J. (2002) 'Communicating with the Body in Performance', in J. Rink (ed.) *Musical Performance: A Guide to Understanding*. Cambridge: Cambridge University Press, 144–52.

Davis, C. B. (1999) 'Performing Theories of Consciousness', *Performance and Consciousness*, 1, 4, 59–72.

Delannoy, L. (1993) *Pres: The Story of Lester Young*. Trans. E. B. Odio. Fayetteville: University of Arkansas Press.

Deleuze, G. (1987) *Cinema 1: The Movement-Image*. Trans. H. Tomlinson and B. Habberjam. Minneapolis: University of Minnesota Press.

____ (1989) *Cinema 2: The Time-Image*. Trans. H. Tomlinson and B. Habberjam. Minneapolis: University of Minnesota Press.

Deleuze, G. and F. Guattari (1994) *A Thousand Plateaus: Capitalism and Schizophrenia*. Trans. B. Massumi. Minneapolis: University of Minnesota Press.

DeVeaux, S. (1997) *The Birth of Bebop: A Social and Musical History*. Berkeley: University of California Press.

Dickinson, K. (2007) 'Music Video and Synaesthetic Possibility', in R. Beebe and J. Middleton (eds) *Medium Cool: Music Videos from Soundies to Cell Phones*. Durham: Duke University Press, 13–29.

Dohrn-van Rossum, G. (1996) *History of the Hour: Clocks and Modern Temporal Orders*. Trans. Thomas Dunlap. Chicago: Chicago University Press.

Doherty, T. (1999) *Pre-Code Hollywood: Sex, Immorality, and Insurrection in American Cinema, 1930–1934*. New York: Columbia University Press.

Donahue, A. (2008) 'Jonas Brothers to Star in 3-D Concert Film', *Billboard*, 6 May. Available at: http://www.billboard.com/bbcom/news/article_display.jsp?vnu_content_id=10037993232 (accessed 10 January 2009).

Dykstra, K. (2005) 'Docurama on the Rise', *Independent*, 1 December, 36–9.

Eisenstein, S. (1994) *Selected Works Volume 2: Towards a Theory of Montage*. Eds. M. Glenny and R. Taylor. Trans. M. Glenny. London: British Film Institute.

Eliot, T. S. (1971) *The Complete Poems and Plays, 1909–1950*. New York: Harcourt Brace.

Ellis, J. C. and B. A. McLane (2005) *A New History of Documentary Film*. New York: Continuum.

Fraim, J. (1996) *Spirit Catcher: The Life and Art of John Coltrane*. West Liberty, OH: GreatHouse.

Fonarow, W. (1997) 'The Spatial Organization of the Indie Music Gig', in K. Gelder and S. Thornton (eds) *The Subcultures Reader*. London: Routledge, 360–9.

Foucault, M. (1984) 'Nietzsche, Genealogy, History', in P. Rabinow (ed.) *The Foucault Reader*. Trans. D. F. Bouchard and S. Simon. New York: Pantheon Books, 76-100.

Frith, S. (1996) *Performing Rites: On the Value of Popular Music*. Cambridge, MA: Harvard University Press.

Gabbard, K. (1996) *Jammin' at the Margins: Jazz and the American Cinema*. Chicago: University of Chicago Press.

____ (1999) 'Evidence: Monk as Documentary Subject', *Black Music Research Journal*, 19, 207–55.

Gendron, B. (2002) *Between Montmartre and the Mudd Club*. Chicago: University of Chicago Press.

Gilman, S. L. (1996) *Smart Jews: The Construction of the Image of Jewish Superior Intelligence*. Lincoln: University of Nebraska Press.

Gioia, T. (1988) *The Imperfect Art: Reflections on Jazz and Modern Culture*. Oxford: Oxford University Press.

____ (1997) *The History of Jazz*. Oxford: Oxford University Press.

Godlovitch, S. (1998) *Musical Performance: A Philosophical Study*. London: Routledge.

Godøy, R. I (1997) 'Knowledge in Music Theory by Shapes of Musical Objects and Sound-Producing Actions', in M. Leman (ed.) *Music, Gestalt, and Computing: Studies in Cognitive and Systematic Musicology*. Berlin: Springer-Verlag, 89–102.

Godøy, R. I and M. Leman (2009) 'Why Study Musical Gestures', in R. I. Godoy and M. Leman (eds) *Musical Gestures: Sound, Movement, and Meaning*. New York: Routledge, 3–11.

Goodman, N. (1976) *Languages of Art*. Cambridge: Hackett.

Gracyk, T. (1996) *Rhythm and Noise: An Aesthetics of Rock*. Durham: Duke University Press.

Grant, B. K. (2003) 'From Obscurity in Ottawa to Fame in Freedomland: Lonely Boy and the Cultural Meaning of Paul Anka', in J. Leach and J. Sloniowski (eds) *Candid Eyes: Essays on Canadian Documentaries*. Toronto: University of Toronto Press, 48–60.

Grierson, J. (1971) *Grierson on Documentary*. Forsyth Hardy (ed.). New York: Praeger.

Gunning, T. (1990) 'Cinema of Attractions: Early Film, Its Spectator and the Avant-Garde', in T. Elsaesser (ed.) *Early Cinema: Space Frame Narrative*. London: British Film Institute, 56–62.

Gurian, A. (2004) 'Thoughts on Shirley Clarke and the TP Videospace Troupe', *Millennium Film Journal*, 42. Available at: http://mfj-online.org/journalPages/mfj42/gurianpage.html (accessed 9 January 2009).

Hall, J. (1998) '"Don't You Ever Just Watch?": American Cinema Verité and *Dont Look Back*', in B. K. Grant and J. Sloniowski (eds) *Documenting the Documentary*. Detroit: Wayne State University Press, 223–37.

Hebdige, D. (1979) *Subculture: The Meaning of Style*. London: Routledge.

Hegel, G. W. F. (1956) *The Philosophy of History*. Trans. J. Sibree. New York: Dover.

____ (1975) *Aesthetics: Lectures on Fine Art Vol II*. Trans. T. M. Knox. Oxford: Clarendon Press.

Helmholtz, H. von (1971) 'The Physiological Causes of Harmony in Music', in Russell Kahl (ed.) *Selected Writings of Hermann von Helmholtz*. Middletown: Wesleyan University Press, 75-108.

Henderson, D. (2008) *'Scuse Me While I Kiss the Sky: Jimi Hendrix – Voodoo Child*. New York: Atria Books.

Hindemith, P. (1968) *The Craft of Musical Composition*. Trans. A. Mendel. New York: Schott.

Holland, B. (2008) 'When Histrionics Undermine the Music and the Pianist', *New York Times*, 6 February, Section E, 1, 8.

Houle. G. (1987) *Meter in Music, 1600–1800: Performance, Perception, and Notation*. Bloomington: Indiana University Press.

Issari, M. A. and D. A. Paul (1979) *What is Cinema Verité?* Metuchen: Scarecrow Press.

Jacobs, L. (1979) 'The Turn Toward Conservatism', in L. Jacobs (ed.) *The Documentary Tradition Second Edition*. New York: Norton.

James, D. E. (1996) *Power Misses: Essays Across (Un)Popular Culture*. London: Verso.

Jung, F. (2004) 'Fireside Chat with Archie Shepp', *Jazzweekly.com*. 21 February Available at http://www.jazzweekly.com/interviews/shepp.htm (accessed 24 February 2010).

Kaemmer, J. E. (1993) *Music in Human Life: Anthropological Perspectives on Music*. Austin: University of Texas.

Kahn, D. (1999) *Noise, Water, Meat: A History of Sound in the Arts*. Cambridge: MIT Press.

Kant, I. (1987) *Critique of Judgment*. Trans. W. S. Pluhar. Indianapolis: Hackett.

Karlin, F. and R. Wright (1990) *On the Track: A Guide to Contemporary Film Scoring*. London: Routledge.

Kellogg, E. W. (1955) 'History of Sound Motion Pictures', *Journal of the Society of Motion Picture Television Engineers*, 64, 356–74.

Kermode, M. (2006) 'Pop Music and Festival Films', in L. R. Williams and M. Hammond (eds) *Contemporary American Cinema*. New York: McGraw-Hill, 80–3.

Kipnis, J. (2005) 'Music category exempt from DVD sales slowdown', *Billboard*, 117, 10.

Kracauer, S. (1960) *Theory of Film: The Redemption of Physical Reality*. Princeton, NJ: Princeton University Press.

Kramer, L. (2002) *Musical Meaning: Toward a Critical History*. Berkeley: University of California Press.

Krasner, D. (ed.) (2000) *Method Acting Reconsidered: Theory, Practice, Future*. New York: St. Martins.

Kreul, J. (2004) 'New, New Cinema: The Independent Film Community and the Underground Crossover, 1950–1970', unpublished PhD dissertation, University of Wisconsin.

Kuleshov, L. (1974) *Kuleshov on Film: Writings*. Berkeley: University of California Press.

Kurtz, A. (2007) 'The Dozens: Jazz on a Summer's Day', *Jazz.com*. Available at www.jazz.com/dozens/the-dozens-jazz-on-a-summers-day (accessed 23 February 2010).

Lastra, J. (2000) *Sound Technology and the American Cinema: Perception, Representation, Modernity*. New York: Columbia University Press.

Lebrecht, N. (1991) *The Maestro Myth: Great Conductors in the Pursuit of Power*. Secaucas, NJ: Citadel Press.

Lee, D. (2006) *The Battle of the Five Spot: Ornette Coleman and the New York Jazz Field*. Toronto: Mercury Books.

Leppert, J. (1993) *The Sight of Sound: Music, Representation, and the History of the Body*. Berkeley: University of California Press.

Levertov, D. (1960) 'The Hands', in D. Allen (ed.) *The New American Poetry 1945–1960*. Berkeley: University of California Press, 61.

Levy, S. (2005) 'Easy Riders', *Sight and Sound*, 15, 24–7.

Lewis, G. E. (2008) *A Power Stronger Than Itself: The AACM and American Experimental Music*. Chicago: University of Chicago Press.

Lischi, S. (1997) *The Sight of Time: Films and Videos by Robert Cahen*. Trans. D. Dusinberre. Pisa: ETS.

Lott, E. (1995) 'Double V, Double-Time: Bebop's Politics of Style', in K. Gabbard (ed.) *Jazz Among the Discourses*. Durham, NC: Duke University Press, 243–55.

Loughney, P. (2001) 'Domitor Witnesses the First Complete Public Presentation of the [Dickson Experimental Sound Film]', in R. Abel and R. Altman (eds) *The Sounds of Early Cinema*. Bloomington: Indiana University Press, 215–19.

Luhmann, N. (2000) *Art as a Social System*. Trans. E. M. Knodt. Stanford, CA: Stanford University Press.

Lydon, J. with Keith Zimmerman and Kent Zimmerman (1994) *Rotten: No Irish, No Blacks, No Dogs*. New York: St. Martins Press.

Lyotard, J.-F. (1988) *The Differend: Phrases in Dispute*. Trans. G. Van Den Abbeele. Minneapolis: University of Minnesota Press.

Macey, S. L. (1989) *The Dynamics of Progress: Time, Method, and Measure*. Athens: University of Georgia Press.

Maconie, R. (1997) *The Science of Music*. Oxford: Clarendon Press.

Mailer, N. (1957) 'The White Negro', *Learntoquestion.com*. Available at www.learntoquestion.com/resources/database/archives/003327.html (accessed 23 February 2010).

Mamber, S. (1974) *Cinema Verite in America: Studies in Uncontrolled Documentary*. Cambridge, MA: MIT Press.

Martin, P. J. (1995) *Sounds and Society: Themes in the Sociology of Music*. Manchester: Manchester University Press.

Marcus, G. (1991) *Lipstick Traces: A Secret History of the Twentieth Century*. Cambridge, MA: Harvard University Press.

Marx, K. and F. Engels (1970) *The German Ideology*. New York: International Publishers.

Mathieson, K. (2002) *Cookin': Hard bop and soul jazz, 1954–65*. Edinburgh: Canongate.

Maturana, H. R. and F. J. Varela (1998) *The Tree of Knowledge: The Biological Roots of Human Understanding*. Boston: Shambhala.

McElhaney, J. (2009) *Albert Maysles*. Urbana: University of Illinois Press.

McNeil, L. and G. McCain (1996) *Please Kill Me: The Uncensored Oral History of Punk*. New York: Penguin.

Meadows, E. S. (2003) *Bebop to Cool: Context, Ideology, and Musical Identity*. London: Praeger.

Meigh-Andrews, C. (2006) *A History of Video Art: The Development of Form and Function*. New York: Berg.

Merleau-Ponty, M. (2003) 'Eye and Mind', in Thomas Baldwin (ed.) *Basic Writings*. New York, Routledge, 290–324.

Mitry, J. (1997) *The Aesthetics and Psychology of the Cinema*. Trans. Christopher King. Bloomington: Indiana University Press.

Monk, N. E. and J. Guterman (1990) *12 Days on the Road: The Sex Pistols and America*. New York: William Morrow.

Mungen, A. (2003) 'The Music is the Message: The Day Jimi Hendrix Burned his Guitar', in I. Inglis (ed.) *Popular Music and Film*. London: Wallflower Press, 60–76.

Murray, C. S. (1988) *Crosstown Traffic: Jimi Hendrix and the Post-War Rock 'n' Roll Revolution*. New York: St. Martin's Press.

Naremore, J. (1988) *Acting in the Cinema*. Berkeley: University of California Press.

Neal, M. A. (1999) *What the Music Said: Black Popular Music and Black Public Culture*. London: Routledge.

New American Cinema Group (2000) 'First Statement of the New American Cinema Group', in P. Adams Sitney (ed.) *Film Culture Reader*. New York: Cooper Square Press, 79-83.

Nichols, B. (1991) *Representing Reality: Issues and Concepts in Documentary*. Bloomington: Indiana University Press.

_____ (1994) *Blurred Boundaries: Questions of Meaning in Contemporary Culture*. Bloomington: Indiana University Press.

_____ (2001) *Introduction to Documentary*. Bloomington: Indiana University Press.

Nietzsche, F. (1974) *The Gay Science*. Trans. W. Kaufmann. New York: Vintage Books.

O'Connell, P. J. (1992) *Robert Drew and the Development of Cinema Verite in America*. Carbondale: Southern Illinois University Press.

Ogren, K. J. (1992) *The Jazz Revolution: Twenties America and the Meaning of Jazz*. Oxford: Oxford University Press.

Oppenheim, D. (1968) 'Letter to Shirley Clarke'. Shirley Clarke Papers, archives of the University of Wisconsin.

Panish, J. (1997) *The Color of Jazz: Race and Representation in Postwar American Culture*. Jackson: University of Mississippi.

Pareles, J. (1989) 'Pop View; The Best Way to Hear Jazz Is to See It', *New York Times*, 24 September. Available at: http://query.nytimes.com/gst/fullpage.html?res=950D EED91039F937A1575AC0A96F948260&sec (accessed 26 May 2006).

Parker, J. (2008) Notes to DVD booklet for *Jayne Parker*. British Artists Films.

Parker, J. (2009) 'Woodstock Nation', *The Atlantic*. September. Available at: http://www. theatlantic.com/magazine/archive/2009/09/woodstock-nation/7611/ (accessed 11

November 2011).

Paudras, F. (1988) *Dance of the Infidels: A Portrait of Bud Powell*. New York: Da Capo.

Pearson, R. E. (1992) *Eloquent Gestures: The Transformation of Performance Style in the Griffith Biograph Films*. Berkeley: University of California Press.

Peretti, B.W. (1992) *The Creation of Jazz: Music, Race, and Culture in Urban America*. Urbana: University of Illinois Press.

Plantinga, C. (1997) *Rhetoric and Representation in Nonfiction Film*. Cambridge: Cambridge University Press.

____ (2000) 'American Documentary in the 1980s', in S. Prince (ed.) *A New Pot of Gold: Hollywood Under the Electronic Rainbow, 1980–1989*. Berkeley: University of California Press, 370–89.

Plato (1970) *The Laws*. Trans. T. J. Saunders. London: Penguin.

Porter, E. (1999) '"Dizzy Atmosphere": The Challenge of Bebop', *American Music*, 17, 4, 422–46.

Pozen, W. (1968) Letter to Shirley Clarke. Shirley Clarke Papers, archives of the University of Wisconsin.

Rabinovitz, L. (2003) *Points of Resistance: Women, Power and Politics in the New York Avant-garde Cinema, 1943–1971*. Chicago: University of Chicago Press.

Radano, R. M. (1993) *New Musical Figurations: Anthony Braxton's Cultural Critique*. Chicago: University of Chicago Press.

____ (2003) *Lying up a Nation: Race and Black Music*. Chicago: University of Chicago Press.

Ramachandran, V. S. and S. Blakeslee (1998) *Phantoms in the Brain*. New York: Quill.

Ratliff, B. (2008) 'Jimmy Giuffre, Jazz Musician, Is Dead at 86', *New York Times*, 25 April, Obituaries.

Renov, M. (1993) *Theorizing Documentary*. New York: Routledge.

____ (2004) *The Subject of Documentary*. Minneapolis: University of Minnesota Press.

Rice, S. (1972) 'Shirley Clarke: Image and Images', *Take One*, 7 February, 22.

Rippa, R. (2006) 'Albert Maysles: 50 Years of Reality Cinema'. Online. Available at www.rapportoconfidenziale.org/?p=7016 (accessed 17 November 2010).

Roby, S. (2002) *Black Gold: The Lost Archives of Jimi Hendrix*. New York: Billboard Books.

Romney, J. (1995) 'Access All Areas: The Real Space of Rock Documentary', in J. Romney and A. Wootton (eds.) *Celluloid Jukebox: Pop Music and the Movies since the 50s*. London: British Film Institute, 82–93.

Rosenthal, D. H. (1992) *Hard Bop: Jazz and Black Music, 1955–1965*. New York: Oxford University Press.

Rotha, P. (1952) *Documentary Film*. London: Faber and Faber.

Rothman, W. (1996) 'Eternal Verités', in W. Rothman (ed.) *Beyond Document: Essays on Nonfiction Film*. Hanover, NH: Wesleyan University Press, 86–100.

Royce, A. P. (2004) *Anthropology of the Performing Arts*. Walnut Creek, CA: AltaMira

Press.

Ruby, J. (2008) 'A Future for Ethnographic Film?', *Journal of Film and Video*, 60, 5–14.

Russell, R. (1996) *Bird Lives! The High Life & Hard Times of Charlie (Yardbird) Parker*. New York: Da Capo.

Russolo, L. (1913) 'The Art of Noises: Futurist Manifesto', in C. Cox and D. Warner (eds) *Audio Culture: Readings in Modern Music* (2004). Trans. R. Filliou. New York: Continuum, 10–14.

Ryle, G. (1949) *The Concept of Mind*. Chicago: University of Chicago Press.

_____ (1971) 'The Thinking of Thoughts: What is Le Penseur Doing?', in *Gilbert Ryle: Collected Papers*. New York: Barnes and Noble, 480-496.

Sachs, J. (2005) 'Aristotle: Motion and Its Place in Nature', *Internet Encyclopedia of Philosophy*. Available at www.iep.utm.edu/aris-mot/ (accessed 17 November 2010).

Saunders, D. (2007) *Direct Cinema: Observational Documentary and the Politics of the Sixties*. London: Wallflower Press.

Savage, J. (2001) *England's Dreaming: Anarchy, Sex Pistols, Punk Rock, and Beyond*. New York: St. Martin's Griffin.

Saussine, R. (1954) *Paganini*. Trans. M. Laurie. Westport: Greenwood Press.

Schowalter, D. F. (2000) 'Remembering the Dangers of Rock and Roll: Toward a Historical Narrative of the Rock Festival', *Critical Studies in Media Communication*, 17, 86–102.

Scott, A.O. (2004) 'Heavy Metal Headshrinking and Other Secrets of the Rock 'n' Roll Business', *New York Times*, 9 July, 10.

Scruton, R. (1988) *The Aesthetic Understanding: Essays in the Philosophy of Art and Culture*. South Bend, IN: St. Augustine's Press.

_____ (1997) *The Aesthetics of Music*. Oxford: Oxford University Press.

Shove, P. and B. H. Repp (1995) 'Musical Motion and Performance: Theoretical and Empirical Perspectives', in J. Rink (ed.) *The Practice of Performance*. Cambridge: Cambridge University Press, 55–83.

Sidran, B. (1971) *Black Talk*. New York: Holt, Rhinehart and Winston.

Stern, B. (2000) 'A Summer's Day with Bert Stern' (DVD audio commentary) *Jazz on a Summer's Day*. New York: New Yorker Video.

Taubin, A. (2000) 'Rock and Roll Zapruder'. Essay in DVD booklet for *Gimme Shelter*. Criterion Collection, 5–8.

Teasdale, P. D. (1999) *Videofreex: America's First Pirate TV Station and the Catskills Collective that Turned It On*. New York: Black Dome Press.

Terenzio, M., with S. MacGillivray and T. Okuda (1991) *The Soundies Distributing Corporation of America*. London: McFarland & Company.

Thomas, L. (1995) 'Music and the Black Arts Movement', in K. Gabard (ed.) *Jazz Among the Discourses*. Durham: Duke University Press, 256–74.

Thomson, K. (1985) 'The Continuity System', in D. Bordwell, J. Staiger and K. Thompson (eds) *The Classical Hollywood Cinema: Film Style and Mode of Production to 1960*.

New York: Columbia University Press, 194–213.

Todd, N. P. M. (1995) 'The Kinematics of Musical Expression', *Journal of the Acoustical Society of America*, 97, 3, 1940–9.

Truslit, A. (1993) 'Shaping and Motion in Music', Trans. B. H. Repp. *Pyschology of Music*, 21, 48–72.

Turim, M. (2007) Art/Music/Video.com', in R. Beebe and J. Middleton (eds) *Medium Cool: Music Videos from Soundies to Cellphones*. Durham: Duke University Press, 83–110.

Van Gelder, L. (1987) 'Maysles: Filming the Impossible', *New York Times*, 18 October, 19.

Vernallis, C. (2004) *Experiencing Music Video: Aesthetics and Cultural Context*. New York: Columbia University Press.

Vertov, D. (1985 [1924]) 'We: Variant of a Manifesto', in A. Michelson (ed.) *Kino-Eye: The Writings of Dziga Vertov*. Trans. K. O'Brien. Berkeley: University of California Press, 5–9.

Vogels, J. B. (2005) *The Direct Cinema of David and Albert Maysles*. Carbondale: Southern Illinois University Press.

Wadleigh, M. (2004) 'Film Director Michael Wadleigh: Interview with John Walters', *NHPR*. Available at: www.nhpr.org/node/7381 (accessed 23 February 2010).

Waksman, S. (1999) *Instrument of Desire: The Electric Guitar and the Shaping of Musical Experience*. Cambridge, MA: Harvard University Press.

Ward, M. (1982) 'Shirley Clarke: An Interview', in M. Ward and B. Jenkins (eds) *The American New Wave 1958–67*. Buffalo, NY: Walker Art Center, 18–25.

Waugh, T. (1990) 'Acting to Play Oneself: Notes on Performance in Documentary', in C. Zucker (ed.) *Making Visible the Invisible: An Anthology of Original Essays on Film Acting*. Metuchen, NJ: Scarecrow, 64–91.

West, D. (1996) '"Cinema-verite", nineties style: an interview with Joe Berlinger and Bruce Sinofsky', *Cineaste*, 22, 21–3.

Wilonsky, R. (2004) 'Fab Film: Forty Years Ago, Al Maysles met the Beatles', *Houston Press*, 19 February. Available at: http://www.houstonpress.com/2004-02-19/culture/fab-film/ (accessed 9 January 2009).

Wilson, J. S. (1950) 'Bop at End of Road, Says Dizzy', *Down Beat*, 8 September, 34.

Wilson, P. N. (1999) *Ornette Coleman: His Life and Music*. Berkeley, CA: Berkeley Hills Books.

Winston, B. (1995) *Claiming the Real: The Documentary Film Revisited*. London: British Film Institute.

_____ (2000) *Lies, Damn Lies, and Documentaries*. London: British Film Institute.

Yampolsky, M. (1996) 'Kuleshov's Experiments and the New Anthropology of the Actor', in R. Abel (ed.) *Silent Film*. New Brunswick, NJ: Rutgers University Press, 45–67.

Youngblood, G. (1970) *Expanded Cinema*. New York: E. P. Dutton.

Index